Global Environmental Governance

Foundations of Contemporary Environmental Studies

Global Environmental Governance
by James Gustave Speth and Peter M. Haas

Forthcoming:

Environmental Economics
by Nathaniel Keohane and Sheila Olmstead

Biodiversity, and Ecosystem Conservation Ecology
by Oswald Schmitz

Nature and Human Nature
by Stephen Kellert

Environmental Policy and Law
by Daniel Esty and Douglas Kysar

Environmental Health
by John Wargo

GLOBAL ENVIRONMENTAL GOVERNANCE

James Gustave Speth

Peter M. Haas

WASHINGTON · COVELO · LONDON

Library of Congress Cataloging-in-Publication Data

Speth, James Gustave.
    Global environmental governance / James Gustave Speth, Peter M. Haas.
        p. cm. — (Foundations of contemporary environmental studies)
    Includes bibliographical references and index.
    ISBN 1-59726-080-0 (acid-free paper) — ISBN 1-59726-081-9 (pbk. : acid-free paper)
    1. Environmental economics—International cooperation. 2. Environmental
management—International cooperation. 3. Environmental policy—International
cooperation. 4. Environmental degradation. I. Haas, Peter M. II. Title. III. Series.
    HC79.E5S6653   2006
    333.7—dc22   2006009294

Printed on recycled, acid-free paper ✇

Manufactured in the United States of America
10 9 8 7 6 5

For our children, and theirs.

Table of Contents

Preface

WE ARE PLEASED TO BE ABLE TO OFFER THIS FIRST VOLUME IN THE SERIES, Foundations of Contemporary Environmental Studies. Other volumes will be forthcoming in the months and years ahead. As the field of environmental studies grows and matures, it is becoming the lens through which many fields apply their insights to maintain or improve the quality of life and the natural world around us—an objective increasingly known as sustainability. Each of the volumes in this series presents a concise statement of one of the fundamental components of the emerging science and practice of sustainability. These books are intended both for university instruction—to train tomorrow's citizens—as well as for concerned readers seeking to understand the latest thinking and developments.

The two of us come to this project from very different backgrounds. Speth's career has been more practitioner than scholar; he has held senior positions in the federal government, in the United Nations, and in two environmental organizations over a 35-year period. Haas has conducted extensive academic research on the issues covered in this volume for 25 years and has experience teaching undergraduates for almost that long. We hope our coming together has produced a useful fusion of information and ideas.

Despite our different perspectives, we share a deep concern for the future in which our children and their children will live. As we describe in the chapters that follow, efforts launched by the international community over the past quarter-century to address the 10 most threatening global environmental problems have not been notably successful. Something new and possibly quite different is needed, and needed soon, if we hope to forestall very serious deterioration of the natural assets that sustain human societies and their economies. We have tried to combine our perspectives to provide a book that speaks to both the heart and the mind, since a better world depends on passionate and informed debate.

We hope that this book will portray vividly what the major global environmental challenges are, what the community of nations and others have done to confront these challenges, and where efforts might go from here for a more successful attempt at global environmental governance.

We also hope to inform both the efforts of professionals working to address our environmental problems as well as to help train the next generation of actors on the global environmental stage. To this end we have included at the end of this volume two useful resources. The first is a list of books that readers can consult for more detailed information on the specific domestic and international policies needed to address global environmental challenges such as climate change. The second is a list of study questions intended to encourage critical thinking about these issues. These questions, to which there are no easy answers, should help to spur innovative responses that today's students will need to develop into action if we are to preserve the quality of life on our planet.

Numerous colleagues took the time to provide very thoughtful comments on earlier drafts. They are not responsible for our remaining shortcomings, but we are deeply grateful to them, including: Ben Cashore, Nazli Choucri, Jennifer Clapp, Beth DeSombre, Dan Esty, Steve Kellert, Bill Moomaw, Craig Murphy, Kate O'Neill, Jim Salzman, Oswald Schmitz, Stacy Vandeveer, Norman Vig, Paul Wapner, and, of course, our excellent editor at Island Press, Todd Baldwin.

We also wish to thank the following students for research assistance: Paul Adams, Zuhre Aksoy, Chris Marcoux, Rebecca Root, and Casey Stevens. Sammy Barkin and Katherine Hochstettler were also helpful with detailed information. Amlan Goswami deserves special praise for his work in the early stages, especially on chapter 3, and Sherry Ryan did a marvelous and much appreciated job preparing the manuscript. Cameron Speth and Pam McElwee read the manuscript and suggested numerous improvements in our writing and presentation. We thank them all.

James Gustave Speth
Yale University
New Haven, Connecticut

Peter M. Haas
University of Massachusetts
Amherst, Massachusetts

I

Introduction: Toward
Planetary Stewardship

THERE ARE MORE PEOPLE AND ECONOMIC ACTIVITY ON THE PLANET THAN ever before, and the environmental consequences of actions large and small are now more widely felt than ever before. A house constructed in the United States often contains wood imported from fragile tropical ecosystems; the transportation of materials required consumption of polluting fossil fuels; many of the building supplies used in construction release gases that can be toxic to construction workers and to the occupants of the house. Small-scale decisions combine to have larger consequences, in terms of both public health and the broader health of the global environment on which human societies and their economies depend. As the number of people on the planet grows, and their consumer aspirations grow even faster, the collective human footprint on the planet is becoming increasingly heavy and global in scope.

How can we address these global environmental threats? This book investigates the various approaches that the community of nations, environmental groups, international businesses, and organizations have pursued in recent decades. It describes and evaluates the effectiveness of these efforts and, in so doing, shows what principles of governance we can apply to both policymaking and individual choices on behalf of an environmentally sustainable future.

These threats can be examined from global, national, and local perspectives. Each perspective has value, and each receives attention here. Through the global perspective, we can gauge the health of the planet and examine how human societies are interacting with the natural world. At the national level, where territory is controlled by sovereign nations, the most important political decisions are actually made in today's world. At the local level, individuals and communities make choices about what products to buy and what kinds of lives to live, at least those of us fortunate enough to live where such choices are possible. We know the local environmental quality because we see it, breathe it, work and play in it. There is tremendous power in this concreteness but also the potential for confusion if the threats are global—such as climate change—seemingly remote and certainly hard to perceive.

Few people deliberately set out to destroy the environment, although in war and on other occasions such intentional destruction has occurred. Corporate executives, government officials, and citizens don't begin each day with the intent to do environmental damage. People act to reap rewards, and most often the benefits of economic decisions are immediate and gratifying while the costs of these decisions are often borne broadly by others, sometimes others in far parts of the world who have no way of expressing their displeasure, or those in the future who are not yet even born. So we continue to drive inefficient vehicles and keep our houses overly warm in the winter and chillingly cold in the summer, and companies continue to produce gas-guzzling SUVs and generate electricity in outmoded coal-fired power plants—all despite strong warnings that our reliance on fossil fuels—coal, oil, and natural gas—is warming the earth.

These problems are not solved simply by decree; steps must be taken to provide a powerful new set of incentives and disincentives to institutions and individuals whose behavior affects the environment. Creating these incentives and disincentives is conventionally the realm of government, acting at all three levels and wielding powers to tax, spend, and regulate. But funds can also be raised privately without taxation, consumers spend far more than governments, and various means exist to accomplish *de facto* regulation even without governmental authority to coerce. So governance can sometimes be accomplished, up to a point, without governments.

The challenge of the global environment is fundamentally one of effective governance—global environmental governance. This book chronicles and critiques the international community's first attempt to build such an approach, which spanned the quarter century between 1980 and 2005. Of course the story is still unfolding, and there are many lessons yet to be learned. What will happen in the next era remains to be decided.

Global Governance, Environmental and Otherwise

The Commission on Global Governance, writing in its 1995 report, *Our Global Neighborhood,* defined *global governance* as follows:

Governance is the sum of the many ways individuals and institutions, public and private, manage their common affairs. It is a continuing process through which conflicting or diverse interests may be accommodated and co-operative action may be taken. It includes formal institutions and regimes empowered to enforce compliance, as well as informal arrangements that people and institutions either have agreed to or perceive to be in their interest.

At the global level, governance has been viewed primarily as intergovernmental relationships, but it must now be understood as also involving non-governmental organizations (NGOs), citizens' movements, multinational corporations, and the global capital market. Interacting with these are global mass media of dramatically enlarged influence.

From this definition it is clear that, as the Commission notes, "global governance is not global government. . . . We are not proposing movement towards a world government."

The concept of governance is thus broad: it includes governmental actions but also includes other processes, formal and informal, that communities employ to decide what is in their common interest, and how to act collectively.

Global environmental governance is the intersection of global governance with environmental affairs. Global environmental governance includes but is not limited to governance of the global commons. (On global commons, see the box on page 7.)

Commission on Global Governance. 1995. *Our Global Neighborhood.* Oxford: Oxford University Press, 2–3.

Stewardship Assignments: A Thought Experiment

Let us begin with a very global perspective. Can you imagine Earth without people, not today's Earth but an Earth that evolved to the present without us? If you can contemplate such a world with satisfaction rather than sadness—a world with forests of majestic old-growth trees, with oceans brimming over with fish, with clear skies literally darkened by passing flocks of birds, thriving with an awe-inspiring diversity of life and landscape but without people—then you not only have a vivid environmental imagination but, more to the point, you are ready for your first assignment as an environmental steward.

Imagine further that you live on a different planet that also circles Earth's sun. Though your world has become depleted and polluted, you and your people have decided to leave Earth alone—to protect it and all its beauty and let it evolve in its own uninterrupted way. It is enough to know that it is there in all its richness, protected for all time, wild, whole, and beautiful.

Your assignment of protecting the pristine Earth is almost entirely farfetched, but not completely. Consider that on Sunday, September 21, 2003, the space probe *Galileo,* having provided scientists extraordinary amounts of new information about Jupiter's moons, was intentionally incinerated in a fiery crash into Jupiter itself. The National Aeronautics and Space Administration scientists took this unusual step out of concern that organisms from our planet—stowaways on *Galileo*—might still be alive and therefore might contaminate one of Jupiter's moons, where life might already exist waiting to be discovered. A decision had been made to leave Jupiter's moons intact and unpolluted. And in the United States today an area the size of California has been set aside as "forever wild" in a magnificent system of national wilderness areas.

But now imagine that another decision has been made. Your world has just learned that it is going to be demolished to make room for an intergalactic hyperspatial express route. When your people complained to the Hyperspace Planning Council about this planned destruction, you were told that the proposed expressway plan had been duly posted in the local planning department in Alpha Centauri and that the time for public comment had long since expired! (With apologies to *The Hitchhikers Guide to the Galaxy.*)

As a result of these unfortunate developments, your people—all 6.5 billion of you—have now decided to colonize the pristine Earth. Your new assignment as environmental steward is to settle Earth in a way that allows all of you to enjoy a decent standard of living while having the smallest possible impact on Earth's environment.

In contemplating this difficult assignment, two things occur to you right away. First, if you are going to sustain Earth's environment, you had better understand how Earth works: how Earth's abundant species interact among themselves and with the landscape; how Earth's great natural

Sustainable Development and Environmental Sustainability

The concept of sustainable development first emerged in the early 1980s and gained a high level of currency after its prominent inclusion in the 1987 Brundtland Commission report, *Our Common Future*. The definition offered by the Commission attempted to strike a balance between the pressure of continued economic development and the necessity to curtail or reverse the oft-destructive impact of such development upon the environment: "Development that meets the needs and aspirations of the present without compromising the ability to meet those of the future."*

This definition has not been without criticism or alternatives. Nonetheless, it has proved lasting and has provided an important foundation for ongoing debate and discussion of environmental threats and its relationship to economic development.

Environmental sustainability has been defined as "achieving sustainable development patterns and preserving the productive capacity of natural ecosystems for future generations."**

In achieving sustainability, is one merely sustaining the productive system's overall capacity (capital) or is one sustaining each type of capital (industrial, natural, and social)? The former is referred to as weak sustainability; the latter as strong. Neoclassical economists tend toward the former; they take the position that environmental capital can decline if it is replaced by other forms of capital. Ecologists, ecological economists, and environmentalists tend toward the latter. They do not view weak sustainability as sustainable practically or politically.

*The World Commission on Environment and Development. 1987. *Our Common Future*. Oxford: Oxford University Press, 40.

**United Nations Development Programme. 2003. *Human Development Report 2003*. Oxford: Oxford University Press, 123.

cycles of water, oxygen, carbon, nitrogen, and others work together to sustain life; where the areas of greatest species richness and diversity and also the zones of greatest fragility are located. If you hope to disturb Earth minimally, then you have first to understand it. So there is first and foremost a huge science project to be undertaken—the science of environmental sustainability.

Second, you see right away that all the nation-states fleeing your planet together must agree at the outset on a set of principles to guide your

One recent effort on the part of international lawyers to elaborate sustainable development principles for nation-states to consider was the New Delhi Declaration of Principles of International Law Relating to Sustainable Development, developed in 2002 by the International Law Association.

settlement of Earth, to do so in such a way that the planet will provide a lasting home for you and your people. You're not going to want to undertake such a task more than once! Where do you begin?

One recent effort on the part of international lawyers to elaborate sustainable development principles for nation-states* to consider was the New Delhi Declaration of Principles of International Law Relating to Sustainable Development, developed in 2002 by the International Law Association.[1] It provides the following:

- "States are under a duty to manage natural resources, including natural resources within their own territory or jurisdiction, in a rational, sustainable and safe way so as to contribute to the development of their peoples . . and to the conservation and sustainable use of natural resources and the protection of the environment, including ecosystems. States must take into account the needs of future generations in determining the rate of use of natural resources. All relevant actors (including States, industrial concerns and other components of civil society) are under a duty to avoid wasteful use of natural resources and promote waste minimization policies."

- "The protection, preservation and enhancement of the natural environment, particularly the proper management of the climate system, biological diversity and fauna and flora of the Earth, are the common concern of humankind. The resources of outer space and celestial bodies and of the sea-bed, ocean floor and subsoil thereof beyond the limits of national jurisdiction are the common heritage of humankind."

*Nations, nation-states, states, and countries are all used interchangeably here. International law texts typically refer to nations as states, but we will try to refrain from that usage to avoid confusion with the 50 U.S. states.

Common Heritage of Humankind, Common Concern of Humankind, and the Global Commons

Areas outside the sovereignty of nations—the high seas, the seabed, the upper atmospheres, outer space, Antarctica—are frequently referred to as the "global commons." For awhile, for example during the negotiation of the Law of the Sea in the 1970s and early 1980s, it appeared that the resources of the global commons would be governed by an international law principle known as *the common heritage of humankind.* Common heritage resources are those that are owned by all nations, not one; that are managed multilaterally, not unilaterally, with the benefits of that management shared by all; and that are used for peaceful purposes only. Except for very isolated uses, however, all this proved too large a pill for the United States and some other countries to swallow. The use of the common heritage concept in international environmental law is now de minimis.

A weaker concept, *the common concern of humankind,* has gained wide currency. A growing consensus has emerged that, because the planet is ecologically interdependent, humanity has an interest in activities or resources that are wholly within national boundaries. The decision reached with respect to the Biodiversity Convention and the Climate Change Convention is that these treaties address common *concerns* of humankind. Unlike the common heritage concept, common concern does not imply specific legal obligations, but it does signal the openness of the international community to regulate resources that would otherwise be strictly within the control of sovereign nations.

But are these proposed principles of international law sufficiently ambitious and unambiguous to guide the contemplated settlement of Earth? Perhaps, but you may want to consider more demanding requirements. And in any event, such broad principles must be supplemented with specific policies and programs that address such fundamental issues as the growth of human populations, the choice of technologies to be used on Earth, the pattern of human settlements to be allowed, the permitted means of transportation and communication, and so on. Moreover, to deal with the problem of the sovereign nations of your planet cooperating in the settlement of Earth, you may wish to consider far-reaching provisions such as these:

- "The Earth shall be used by all States Parties exclusively for peaceful purposes."

- "In exploring and using the Earth, States Parties shall take measures to prevent the disruption of the existing balance of its environment whether by introducing adverse changes in that environment, by its harmful contamination through the introduction of extra-environmental matter or otherwise."

- The Earth and its natural resources are the common heritage of mankind . . . "

- "The Earth is not subject to national appropriation by any claim of sovereignty, by means of use or occupation, or by any other means."

- "Neither the surface nor the subsurface of the Earth, nor any part thereof of natural resources in place, shall become property of any State, international intergovernmental or non-governmental organization, national organization or non-governmental entity or of any natural person."

These are in fact actual provisions of the Moon Treaty, the 1979 Agreement Governing the Activities of States on the Moon and Other Celestial Bodies, with *Earth* substituted for *moon* in the text.[2] As of 2005, only 11 countries had ratified the 1979 Moon Treaty. No country with a significant space program, including the United States, had ratified it.

In the end there is the question whether it will be possible for 6.5 billion of you to settle Earth and build a world economy that can provide everyone a prosperous standard of living, all the while protecting the treasured natural beauty and bounty of the planet. Whatever the odds of achieving this truly sustainable development on Earth, they are improved if the people and nations undertaking the colonization are at peace not at war, if they are democracies not dictatorships, if their people are well-informed about science and policy choices, if they share deeply the values of social justice and environmental protection and care about the future as well as themselves, if they have a tradition of working together cooperatively to forge common goals and solve mutual problems, and if they enjoy a level of economic development that enables them to spend resources on environmental protection. Do the nations of your world meet these tests? If they cannot agree on fundamental goals and how to realize them, and cooperate successfully among themselves, then their experiment in global governance on the new planet will likely fail.

The Real World: Only One Earth

However difficult planning the sustainable settlement of a pristine planet might be, it is child's play compared with the real-world task we all now face on Earth. As the 1987 World Commission on Environment and Development (the Brundtland Commission) wrote, "the Earth is one but the world is not." How do we achieve environmental sustainability in our world today? The real world's 6.5 billion people are already spread across six continents, settled in geographic patterns that have been determined historically over thousands of years. They work in a $55 trillion world economy (in 2003 U.S. dollars) made possible by technologies designed when the environment was not a concern and obeying price and other market signals that do not take environmental protection into account. They live in nation-states claiming sovereignty within their geographic borders, including the sovereign right to develop the natural resources within those borders as they see fit. These nation-states are divided between rich and poor, democratic and nondemocratic. They are divided by race, religion, ethnicity, language, history, and natural resources. The leading examples of their cooperation among themselves are wartime collaborations, and like the tribes and clans that preceded them, they are prone to conflict to advance their interests as they see them. Since World War II there have been 38 significant international wars (defined as conflicts with more than 1,000 battle deaths and with more than 5 percent of the combatant national troops involved); however, the vast majority of armed conflicts have been civil wars, often of long standing, where the principal casualties are civilians.

The willingness and ability of human societies to wreak havoc on the environment is not new. In 1948 Fairfield Osborn wrote in his prescient book, *Our Plundered Planet,* that, "Man's misuse of the land is very old, going back thousands of years." He chronicled how the "cradle of civilization" in the Middle East gradually became a desert, how Greece and Turkey were deforested, and how the more recent destruction of the American prairie contributed to the Dust Bowl.[3] Historians speak of numerous other civilizations, once mighty like the Khmer Empire in

*As the 1987 World Commission on Environment and Development (the Brundtland Commission) wrote, "the Earth is one but the world is not." How do we achieve **environmental sustainability** in our world today?*

The Tragedy of the Commons

Garrett Hardin, a biologist at the University of California–Santa Barbara, penned "The Tragedy of the Commons" in 1968. The commons, as could be found in old English villages (and in many New England towns), is a parcel of land eligible to be used by all commoners of the village. Hence it is a public good or common-pool resource. The villagers are free to use the land to graze livestock, which they do since it conserves use of their own personal land, which in turn allows them to raise even greater numbers of livestock. However, as Hardin points out: "The rational herdsman concludes that the only sensible course for him to pursue is to add another animal to his herd. And another; and another. . . . But this is the conclusion reached by each and every other rational herdsman sharing a common. Therein is the tragedy. Each man is locked into a system that compels him to increase his herd without limit—in a world that is limited. Ruin is the destination toward which all men rush, each pursuing his own best interest in a society that believes in the freedom of the commons, Freedom in a commons brings ruin to all."*

Hardin's hypotheses are not without their detractors. There is much scholarship and controversy regarding the assumptions of humans and states being purely rational short-term utility-maximizers: "Although tragedies have undoubtedly occurred, it is also obvious that for thousands of years people have self-organized to manage common-pool resources, and users often do devise long-term, sustainable institutions for governing these resources."**

Nonetheless, the tragedy of the commons remains a foundational work in the study of open resource problems.

*Hardin, G. 1968. The tragedy of the commons. *Science* 162:1243.

**Ostrom, E., et al. 1999. Revisting the commons: Local lessons, global challenges. *Science* 284:278.

Southeast Asia or the small tribes that lived on Easter Island in the far Pacific Ocean, that have collapsed, caused in part by destruction of their environments.

Despite these serious depredations in times past, historian J. R. McNeill is correct in asserting that the twentieth century brought something new under the sun. The twentieth century, and particularly the period since World War II, he writes, "shattered the constraints and rough stability of the old economic, demographic and energy regimes." McNeill goes on to write, "In environmental history, the twentieth century qualifies as a peculiar century because of the screeching acceleration of so many of the processes that bring ecological change."[4]

So extraordinary has been this scaling up of environmental impacts in the twentieth century that by 1980 it became obvious that nations would have to collaborate in framing responses to a set of environmental threats of global significance. As noted, we can think of this collective response as the birth of global environmental governance. Why were societies driven to make that effort? What have been the principal means governments have chosen for environmental cooperation? How have they fared? What could be done in a second phase of global environmental governance to correct past and current deficiencies? These are among the key questions taken up in this book.

II

Global-Scale
Environmental Challenges

AN IMPORTANT THING HAPPENED IN 1975 AND THE YEARS IMMEDIATELY following: for the first time, an aroused American public acted as stewards of the global environment.

In 1974, Mario Molina and F. S. Rowland, two University of California scientists, realized that the widespread use of chlorofluorocarbons (CFCs)—highly stable compounds used in aerosol propellants, refrigeration, foam-blowing, and industrial solvents—could damage Earth's stratospheric ozone shield. They hypothesized that CFCs could add chlorine to the stratosphere and, through complex chemical reactions, reduce the amount of strato-spheric ozone, thus weakening the shield and allowing more harmful UVB radiation to reach Earth's surface.[1]

Ozone (O_3) is a variant of oxygen and is present throughout the atmos-phere, but it is concentrated in a belt around the Earth in the stratosphere, 15 to 50 kilometers above Earth's surface. Ozone in the troposphere (near-est the earth's surface) is a component of smog, and it adversely affects human health and plant life. Yet ozone is a valuable component of the upper atmosphere, where it acts as a filter, absorbing wavelengths of ultraviolet radiation (UV-B) that can damage plant and animal life and increase the risk of skin cancers and eye disease.

The Molina-Rowland hypothesis profoundly affected public opinion in the United States, Canada, and the Nordic countries. Environmental ac-tivists and consumers joined forces to stop the use of CFCs in aerosol cans. So powerful was the popular "ban the can" movement that CFC produc-tion took a nosedive, and some major producers of consumer products vol-untarily switched to non-CFC aerosol propellants. Under tremendous pressure to act, including congressional pressure, the Environmental Protection Agency followed in 1978 with a CFC aerosol ban. This act of planetary stewardship underscores that an aroused public is not powerless to affect even a long-term global threat. The ozone depletion issue also exemplifies the truth that the twentieth century brought us across a threshold to a fundamentally new reality. The sheer size of the growing human population, coupled with exponential growth in the world economy and its integration internationally, has given environmental challenges not only a distinctly global cast but also a new urgency.

The Globalization of Environmental Threats

It took all of human history up until 1900 for global population to grow to 1.5 billion. But during the twentieth century, 1.5 billion people were added, on average, every 33 years. Over the last 25 years between 1979 and 2004, global population increased by another 2 billion, from 4.4 billion to 6.4 billion. Virtually all of this growth occurred in the developing world.

The Measure of the Twentieth Century

ITEM	INCREASE FACTOR, 1890s–1990s
World population	4
World urban population	13
World economy	14
Industrial output	40
Energy use	16
Coal production	7
Air pollution	~5
Carbon dioxide emissions	17
Sulfur dioxide emissions	13
Lead emissions to the atmosphere	~8
Water use	9
Marine fish catch	35

McNeill, J. R. 2000. *Something New under the Sun.* (New York: W. W. Norton & Company, 2000), 360.

Population increased fourfold in the last century, but world economic output increased 20-fold, five times faster than population due to increasing affluence. It took all of history to grow the world economy to $7 trillion by 1950 (in 2003 U.S. dollars). Amazingly, it now grows by this amount every 5 to 10 years. In the 40 years between 1965 and 2005, the size of the world economy doubled—and then doubled again. Most of this growth has occurred in the richer industrial countries.

As a result of this phenomenal expansion, especially the growth of economic activity and rising human consumption, environmental costs have mounted exponentially. Simultaneously, concerns that were once strictly local, such as clearing of forests and pollution from burning fuels, have become global challenges. As early as 1957 Roger Revelle, a famous oceanographer, observed that human societies are conducting a large-scale geophysical experiment of a kind that could not have happened in the past nor be reproduced in the future. In 1989, the environmental writer Bill McKibben declared "the end of nature," by which he meant the end of our thinking about nature as an entity or force independent of *Homo sapiens*.[2] Although previously we might have considered the "forces of nature" as largely free of human influence, the twentieth century brought us a new condition. Human influences on the environment are now everywhere, affecting all natural systems and cycles, all the oceans, and every continent.

Recently, scientists have been sounding alarms with greater frequency and urgency. Ecologist Jane Lubchenco, in her 1998 address as president of the American Association for the Advancement of Science, made the following call from the rostrum: "The conclusions . . . are inescapable: during the last few decades, humans have emerged as a new force of nature. We are modifying physical, chemical, and biological systems in new ways, at faster rates, and over larger spatial scales than ever recorded on Earth. Humans have unwittingly embarked upon a grand experiment with our planet. The outcome of this experiment is unknown, but has profound implications for all of life on Earth."[3]

In 1992 1,700 of the world's top scientists, including a majority of Nobel Prize winners, issued a plea for more attention to environmental problems: "The earth is finite. Its ability to absorb wastes and destructive effluents is finite. Its ability to provide food and energy is finite. Its ability to provide for growing numbers of people is finite. Moreover, we are fast approaching many of the earth's limits. Current economic practices that damage the environment, in both developed and underdeveloped nations, cannot be continued without the risk that vital global systems will be damaged beyond repair."[4]

As you realized in the thought experiment (chap. 1) about how you might go about colonizing a pristine Earth, bringing human societies into a sustainable relationship with natural systems is no simple matter. Environmental problems are not just problems of science and technology but are economic and political problems as well. Yet the burden of environmental management now falls squarely on our shoulders. Scientist Peter Vitousek and his coauthors made this point in a 1997 article in *Science:* "Humanity's dominance of Earth means that we cannot escape responsibility for managing the planet. . . . Maintaining populations, species, and ecosystems in the face of those changes, and maintaining the flow of goods and services they provide humanity, will require active management for the foreseeable future."[5]

Whether we like it or not, we are now at the planetary controls and must make the hard choices necessary to address global environmental challenges.

What makes an environmental threat global in scale? Human societies have generated four types of environmental challenges that give rise to the need for collective action among nations. One is abuses of the global commons—the high seas and the upper atmosphere, for example—areas of the planet that are outside the jurisdiction of any particular country. Second is widespread transboundary pollution or similar impacts of one country on another. Interference with shared wildlife corridors and appropriation of shared freshwater resources can also fall into this category, as can the subtle migration of toxic chemicals. Third is a large and often problematic category of activities that threaten local environmental assets of concern to many governments and citizens outside the country where those threats may occur. People everywhere have a stake in the fate of great natural treasures such as the Grand Canyon (once slated for damming and flooding), the Brazilian Pantanal, and the megafauna of the African plains. Just as real is our common stake in the fate of the planet's biological resources—for example, global forests, genetic materials, and ecosystem services. The loss of even very local soil and water supplies that support food production can give rise to crises of international concern. Finally, there are those environmental problems that are strictly local and national but so widely shared that nations may choose to tackle them in concert. Local air and water pollution could be addressed in this way, as could hazardous waste cleanup, but the principal examples of international efforts in this category involve agreements to share information.

If this is the general picture, what specifically are the major environmental challenges we face as planetary stewards? This chapter focuses on 10 major global environmental threats, as identified in the past 30 years of scientific work on the subject. It concludes by addressing the underlying forces giving rise to these threats.

Findings of the Millennium Ecosystem Assessment

The Millennium Ecosystem Assessment was a massive four-year effort involving 1,360 scientists and other experts worldwide to assess conditions and trends regarding the world's ecosystems. At the conclusion of this unprecedented effort in 2005, the board governing the assessment issued the following statement: "Nearly two thirds of the services provided by nature to humankind are found to be in decline worldwide. In effect, the benefits reaped from our engineering of the planet have been achieved by running down natural capital assets. "In many cases, it is literally a matter of living on borrowed time. By using up supplies of fresh groundwater faster than they can be recharged, for example, we are depleting assets at the expense of our children. . . . Unless we acknowledge the debt and prevent it from growing, we place in jeopardy the dreams of citizens everywhere to rid the world of hunger, extreme poverty, and avoidable disease—as well as increasing the risk of sudden changes to the planet's life-support systems from which even the wealthiest may not be shielded. We also move into a world in which the variety of life becomes ever more limited. The simpler, more uniform landscapes created by human activity have put thousands of species under threat of extinction, affecting both the resilience of natural services and less tangible spiritual or cultural values.

"Yet this need not be a counsel of despair. The natural balance sheet we bequeath to future generations depends on choices made at every level and in every corner of the planet—from the head of a village in Bangladesh to a corporation board in a New York skyscraper; from international gatherings of finance ministers to consumers in a Brazilian furniture store."*

*Millennium Ecosystem Assessment Board. March 2005. Statement from the Board. In *Living Beyond Our Means: Natural Assets and Human Well-Being*, 5.

Ten Major Global Environmental Challenges

Accompanying the twentieth century's vast economic expansion have been two categories of change of enormous consequence for the natural environment. First is the dramatic increase in the consumption of the earth's natural resources, principally the so-called renewable resources—the forests, the air, the soils, the fish and animal life, the freshwater. Renewable resources have been appropriated by humans at rates far in excess of sustainable yields. (In an ironic twist, the supply of the earth's nonrenewable resources—principally the fossil fuels and the nonfuel minerals—originally thought to be most subject to scarcities, have thus far been regularly available.)

The second development has been the exponential growth of what we have come to call pollution. Pollution is a case of too much of something in the wrong place. In appropriate quantities, many potential pollutants are beneficial. For example, phosphates and nitrates are plant nutrients essential to life. Too much of these nutrients in aquatic systems, however, and

---

Driving Pollution: What's Happened in the United States since the First Earth Day?

Number of passenger cars in the U.S. in 1970—89.2 million
  in 2003—135.7 million

Miles of paved roads in the U.S. in 1970—1.7 million
  in 2003—2.6 million

Kilowatt-hours of electricity used in the U.S. in 1970—1535 billion
  in 2005—3837 billion

Barrels of petroleum consumed per day in the U.S. in 1970—14.7 million
  in 2005—20.9 million

Municipal solid waste generated per person per day in the U.S. in 1970—
  3.3 pounds
  in 2005—4.4 pounds

Square footage of average new U.S. single-family home in 1970—1500 sq. ft.
  in 2003—2330 sq. ft.

Grist Magazine, 22 April, 2005.

plant growth and decay sap the water of vital oxygen needed by fish and other organisms in the water. Eutrophication is the result. Or take the case of carbon dioxide (CO_2). If it were not for this compound occurring naturally in the atmosphere, our planet would be a frozen wasteland. The CO_2 creates a greenhouse blanket, keeping heat in to warm our atmosphere. Yet, the buildup of too much CO_2 from fossil fuel burning and other sources now threatens to alter the planet's climate and disrupt both ecosystems and human communities.

Today, pollution is occurring on an unprecedented scale worldwide. It is pervasive, affecting in some way virtually everyone and everything on the globe, from CO_2 in our atmosphere, to polychlorinated biphenyl (PCB) in our bodies, to acid rain on our land.

It is the combination of these developments—high demands on renewable resources and large-scale pollution—that has given rise to the major global threats we now face. In this book we will focus on what we see as the 10 principal threats:

- Acid rain and regional-scale air pollution

- Ozone depletion by chlorofluorocarbons and other industrial and agricultural chemicals

- Global warming and climate change due to the increase in "greenhouse gases" in the atmosphere

- Deforestation, especially in the tropics

- Land degradation due to desertification, erosion, compaction, salinization, and other factors

- Freshwater pollution and scarcities

- Marine threats, including overfishing, habitat destruction, acidification, and pollution

- Threats to human health from persistent organic pollutants and heavy metals

- Declines in biodiversity and ecosystem services through loss of species and ecosystems

- Excessive nitrogen production and overfertilization

Global Environmental Threats

Trend	Overuse of Renewable Resources	Pollution		
Effects of Trend*	Biotic Impoverishment Resource Scarcity	Toxification and Threats to Public Health	Atmospheric Change	Chemical Imbalances in Ecosystems
Issues	Marine Losses Desertification Deforestation Freshwater System Decline Biodiversity Loss	Persistent Toxic Chemicals	Ozone Depletion Climate Change	Acid Rain Nitrogen Excess

*Interactive effects are possible between the loss of renewable resources and pollution. Pollution impoverishes natural systems, and biotic impoverishment can make natural systems more vulnerable to pollution.

We can frame these 10 threats in terms of our two previously identified overall trends: overuse and misuse of renewable resources and the increase in pollution, as is presented in the table above.

Collectively, these 10 concerns are seriously threatening Earth's natural endowment, productivity, and habitability, including the services natural ecosystems provide to human societies. The following sections of this chapter describe these threats and indicate their scope and significance. More on the specific national and international policies needed to address each of these challenges can be found in Further Readings.

Many of the examples cited in this chapter involve the United States. The United States exemplifies much of the environmental neglect that characterizes today's times. The United States is not alone in neglecting the environmental effects of its activities, but, as the world's largest economy and major superpower, the United States is a country to which many others turn for leadership and a role model and, due to its size, the effects of U.S. decisions often have international impacts. The Environmental Sustainability index, following, provides a snapshot of the United States' performance in a comparative perspective.

Environmental Sustainability Index (in descending order of national sustainability)

ESI Rank	Country	ESI Score	ESI Rank	Country	ESI Score	ESI Rank	Country	ESI Score
1	Finland	75.1	11	Brazil	62.2	137	Yemen	37.3
2	Norway	73.4	31	Germany	56.9	138	Kuwait	36.6
3	Uruguay	71.8	33	Russia	56.1	139	Trin. & Tob.	36.3
4	Sweden	71.7	36	France	55.2	140	Sudan	35.9
5	Iceland	70.8	45	U.S.A.	52.9	141	Haiti	34.8
6	Canada	64.4	65	U.K.	50.2	142	Uzbekistan	34.4
7	Switzerland	63.7	93	S. Africa	46.2	143	Iraq	33.6
8	Guyana	62.9	95	Mexico	46.2	144	Turkmenistan	33.1
9	Argentina	62.7	101	India	45.2	145	Taiwan	32.7
10	Austria	62.7	133	China	38.6	146	North Korea	29.2

The Environmental Sustainability Index (ESI) ranks 146 countries based on 21 "indicators" of pollution control and natural resource management. Each of these indicators derives from between 2 and 12 variables. For instance, "air quality" is a function of data sets that gauge levels of NO_x, SO_2, particulates, and indoor air quality. The rankings (available for each indicator and variable as well as on an overarching basis) permit benchmarking of national performance against a variety of relevant peer groups—highlighting leaders and laggards and providing a mechanism for identifying "best practices."

The ESI (available at www.yale.edu/esi) has proven to be a valuable policy tool with millions of policymakers, journalists, NGOs, and other interested parties having viewed the website. The index provides a way to put environmental performance in context. ESI creator Daniel Esty has observed that whenever the ESI is discussed in Europe, people are shocked at how high the United States ranks. But in the United States, people are shocked at the low U.S. rank. He believes this reflects the fact that the United States does very well on some issues, such as providing safe drinking water, and very poorly on others, such as controlling greenhouse gases.

Acid Rain and Regional Air Pollution

Before acid rain, most people viewed air pollution as primarily a local, urban event. In fact, the atmosphere can transport many air pollutants hundreds of miles before returning them to Earth's surface. While these pollutants are being picked up and moved, the atmosphere acts as a chemical laboratory, transforming the pollutants as they interact with other substances, moisture, and solar energy. Emissions of sulfur and nitrogen oxides, primarily from fossil fuel combustion such as coal-fired power plants, can be transformed chemically in the atmosphere into sulfuric and nitric acids. These acids then come back to Earth's surface through deposition, primarily through rain, giving us the popular term *acid rain*.

*Emissions of sulfur and nitrogen oxides, primarily from fossil fuel combustion such as coal-fired power plants, can be transformed chemically in the atmosphere into sulfuric and nitric acids. These acids then come back to Earth's surface through deposition, primarily through rain, giving us the popular term **acid rain**.*

Acid rain can cause damage to buildings and exposed metals, eating through surfaces over time, but its impacts on the natural environment have attracted by far the most concern. When these acids come down in wet or dry deposition and pollute lakes and rivers, they change these water bodies' pH balances. Increasing acidity has enormous ramifications for fish and aquatic plants, and thousands of lakes in the United States and Europe have essentially "died" from excessive acid (low pH). Acidity can also affect some forests and soils adversely.

Despite three decades of efforts to reduce sulfur and nitrogen oxide pollution, data from the United States indicate little actual recovery of lakes and soils. It has become clear to many that further cuts in pollutants will be needed for full ecological recovery of these ecosystems.

Although acid deposition is still seen as the primary atmospheric agent damaging aquatic ecosystems, other air pollutants, including smog, can join in contributing to crop damage and forest problems. Smog is formed when nitrogen oxides and volatile hydrocarbons react in the presence of sunlight to produce ozone and other photochemical oxidants. For example, air pollution has been implicated in large-scale forest die-offs in southwestern China, and the World Bank estimates that the cost of air pollution in China's forests and crops exceeds $5 billion annually. Japan, India, the Republic of Korea, and Thailand also have regions with serious pollution damage to crops and forests.

Acid rain is also a classic transborder pollution problem. Examples of regions with transboundary acidification include the United States–Canada, Europe, and China–Japan.

SOUNDINGS • Reuters News Service

BOOMING CHINA AWASH IN "OUT OF CONTROL" ACID RAIN

BEIJING, NOVEMBER 30, 2004 — China's explosive economic growth is outpacing environmental protection efforts, leaving the country awash in "out of control" acid rain, the China Daily said Tuesday.

Acid rain fell on more than 250 cities nationwide and caused direct annual economic losses of 110 billion yuan ($13.3 billion), equal to nearly three percent of the country's gross domestic product, the state-run newspaper said.

"The regional acid rain pollution is still out of control and even worse in some southern cities," Wang Jian, an official with the State Environmental Protection Administration, was quoted as saying.

Two major causes were the rapidly growing number of cars and increasing consumption of cheap, abundant coal as the country struggles to cope with energy shortages and meet power demand.

China is the world's largest source of soot and sulphur dioxide (SO_2) emissions from coal, which fires three-quarters of the country's power plants.

More than 21 million tonnes of SO_2 were discharged in China in 2003, up 12 percent from the year earlier, the paper said.

"It is estimated that the country will consume more than 1.8 billion tonnes of coal in 2005, emitting an additional six million tonnes of SO_2," Wang said.

The paper said the government was planning steps to rein in the problem, including setting quotas for SO_2 emissions from thermal power plants and urging them to install desulphurisation facilities, though Wang admitted earlier efforts had led to no obvious improvements.

Ozone Depletion

As noted at the outset of this chapter, the Molina–Rowland research sparked an international response. The United States, Canada, and Sweden first banned inessential uses of CFC propellants, and several other countries followed suit. World production of the two major CFCs decreased in the late 1970s, but then increased again due to nonaerosol uses. Nations acted in concert in 1985 when they adopted a landmark treaty, the Vienna Convention for the Protection of the Ozone Layer. This convention and its better-known progeny, the 1987 Montreal Protocol, have now required the virtual elimination of CFCs and other ozone-destroying chemicals in the industrial countries, and the process is now moving to focus primarily on the devel-

SOUNDINGS • Associated Press

NO EVIDENCE OZONE LAYER IS RECOVERING, SCIENTISTS SAY

PRAGUE, CZECH REPUBLIC, NOVEMBER 22, 2004—Mexico's Nobel Prize-winning chemist Mario Molina said Friday that despite recent measures scientists still don't have evidence that the ozone layer is recovering.

"We need a big signal before we can tell unambiguously that the ozone layer . . . is recovering," Molina told reporters ahead of the 16th Meeting of the Parties to the Montreal Protocol on Substances that Deplete the Ozone Layer, an annual event where politicians and scientists make adjustments to a global treaty requiring nations to stop using chemicals that destroy the ozone layer . . .

One of the major chemicals still to be phased out was methyl bromide, "a significant contributor" to the ozone layer destruction, Molina said.

Under the protocol, wealthy nations are to eliminate production of methyl bromide completely. . . . However, countries that say they have a critical need for methyl bromide and have no alternatives can seek exemptions.

Delegates to the five-day meeting, which begins in Prague on Monday, have to decide on exemptions for 2006. The United States and 12 other countries are to seek exemptions for that year.

The U.S. government has argued in the past that exemptions from the treaty were needed to avoid disrupting agricultural markets.

At the last year's meeting in Nairobi, Kenya, the U.S. delegation asked to increase by more than 8 percent production of the fumigant used to control insects, nematodes, weeds and pathogens.

Negotiators from the European Union and poor countries at that meeting called the proposed increase too high and refused to agree to the exemption.

In April, Republicans in the House of Representatives promoted a bill that would let the United States ignore the treaty and allow U.S. production of methyl bromide to continue even if other countries don't agree.

oping countries, with an ultimate goal of eliminating the remaining emissions. Scientists estimate that the ozone layer could recover by midcentury if necessary actions are taken, but the recovery process has hardly begun today.

Climate Disruption

Global climate change is the most threatening of the major global change issues. It is also the most complex and controversial. We know that the "greenhouse effect" works: without the naturally occurring heat-trapping gases in Earth's atmosphere, the planet would be about 30°C cooler on average—an iceball rather than a life-support system. The problem arises because human activities have now sharply increased the presence of greenhouse gases in the atmosphere. These gases prevent the escape of Earth's infrared radiation into space. In general, the more gases, the greater the atmosphere's heat-trapping capacity.

The atmospheric concentration of carbon dioxide, the principal greenhouse gas, has increased by a third over the preindustrial level due principally to the use of fossil fuels (coal, oil, natural gas) and to large-scale deforestation. Carbon dioxide in the atmosphere is now at its highest level in over 420,000 years. The concentration of methane (CH_4), another greenhouse gas, is about 150 percent above preindustrial levels. Methane accumulates from the use of fossil fuels, cattle raising, rice growing, and landfill emissions. Atmospheric nitrous oxide (N_2O) concentrations are also up due to fertilizer use, cattle feed lots, and the chemical industry, and it is also an infrared-trapping gas. A number of specialty chemicals in the halocarbon family, including the CFCs of ozone-depletion fame, are also potent greenhouse gases.

What are the consequences of the buildup of these gases? One authoritative report on the subject was issued in 2002 by the U.S. National Academy of Sciences (NAS), responding to a request of the Bush administration. The NAS report reached the conclusion that, indeed, greenhouse gases are accumulating in Earth's atmosphere as a result of human activities. These gases are contributing to rising temperatures, about 1°F global average rise in the twentieth century, and these warming trends could increase by 2.5°F to 10.5°F in this century. The NAS report went on to note that global temperature would continue to rise well into the next century even if the levels of greenhouse gases in the atmosphere were stabilized much earlier.[6] These conclusions broadly conform to the current scientific consensus reflected in the work of the Intergovernmental Panel on Climate Change, the international scientific body responsible for providing authoritative policy relevant advice on climate change.

The likely direct consequences of this phenomenon include a warmer and wetter planet (with greater warming toward the poles), changes in precipitation patterns leading to more floods and droughts, more severe hurricanes and cyclones, and significant sea level rise. Although the specific effects that you or I are likely to encounter are hard to predict, some models now project that by the end of this century climate change will make it impossible for about half the American landscape to sustain the plant and animal communities now found there. While there will be some activities in certain regions that could benefit from modest climate change, there could also be consequences of great seriousness. The following possibilities were noted in recent surveys:

- Significant increases in the geographic range and incidence of insect borne diseases, particularly malaria and dengue, in the tropics and subtropics. In 2004 the World Health Organization (WHO) estimated an annual human toll of 150,000 lives already lost due to climate change.

- Increased risk of hunger and famine for many of the world's poorest people who depend on traditional agricultural systems and coral fisheries.

- The displacement by rising sea levels of tens of millions of people from small island states and the low-lying delta areas of Egypt, Bangladesh, and China, among others. As Alaskan permafrost melts, Inuit villages are already having to be moved inland. Beaches, coastal marshes, and near-coast development could also be severely affected.

- Shifts in the distribution, structure, and functioning of terrestrial and aquatic ecosystems, and potentially irreversible changes such as loss of biodiversity and forests in national parks and protected areas.

- Decreased amounts of precipitation in many arid and semiarid areas, and decreased water supply in areas that depend on melting snow and ice from glaciers.

Although many people assume that climate change is happening gradually, as Earth's temperature slowly rises, the buildup of greenhouse gases may in fact lead to abrupt and sudden, not gradual, changes. A National Academy of Sciences report in 2002 concluded that global climate change could have *rapid* impacts: "Recent scientific evidence shows that major and widespread climate changes have occurred with startling speed. . . . [G]reenhouse warming and other human alterations of the earth system may increase the possibility of large, abrupt, and unwelcome regional or global climatic events."[7]

Scientists at the Woods Hole Oceanographic Institution and others believe that a potential danger is the disruption of ocean currents such as the Gulf Stream. Fossil evidence shows that the Gulf Stream has shut down in the past and pushed the North Atlantic region into a dramatically cooler era. Today's computer models suggest that a shutdown of the Gulf Stream would produce winters twice as cold as the worst winters on record in the eastern United States.

What might cause this disruptive regional cooling? Global warming and other factors are melting northern ice and causing a dramatic increase in freshwater released into the North Atlantic ocean. This "freshening" is well under way. Indeed, according to the Woods Hole scientists, it is "the largest and most dramatic oceanic change ever measured in the era of modern instruments."[8] The mechanisms by which this extra freshwater could disrupt the Gulf Stream are complicated, but basically the fresher water could block the Gulf Stream's release of heat and disrupt the ocean currents that pull the warm waters of the stream northward. Strangely, therefore, global warming could lead to regional cooling, both very disruptive. This possibility was greatly exaggerated in the disaster film, *The Day After Tomorrow.*

There is little doubt that the process of human-induced global warming has begun. Ice is melting at the poles and glaciers are retreating; spring is arriving earlier; and ranges of various species are shifting. Meanwhile, the process of reducing greenhouse gas emissions has hardly started. Global carbon dioxide emission climbed by 22 percent between 1980 and 2000.

One of the most comprehensive studies of the regional impact of climate change is the 2004 Arctic Climate Impact Assessment, a joint effort of the eight Arctic nations, including the United States.[9] It concluded that the Arctic is warming much more rapidly than previously known, at nearly twice the rate as the rest of the globe, and increasing greenhouse gases from human activities will likely make it warmer still. In Alaska, western Canada, and eastern Russia, average winter temperatures have increased as much as 3 to 4°C in the past 50 years and are projected to rise 4 to 7°C over the next 100 years. Warming over Greenland could melt the Greenland ice sheet, gradually contributing to global sea-level rise. Over the long term, Greenland contains enough melt water to eventually raise sea level by about 23 feet. The report makes clear that Arctic developments could affect societies far away from the region by contributing to a rise in sea level, adding positive feedback that accelerates warming, and disrupting ocean currents, including the Gulf Stream.

SOUNDINGS • Reuters News Service

ANTARCTIC GLACIERS IN RETREAT FROM CLIMATE CHANGE

LONDON, APRIL 22, 2005—Most of the glaciers on the Antarctic peninsula are in headlong retreat because of climate change, a leading scientist said on Thursday.

An in-depth study using aerial photographs spanning the past half century of all 244 marine glaciers on the west side of the finger-like peninsula pointing up to South America found that 87 percent of them were in retreat—and the speed was rising.

"Regional warming is the strongest single factor in this retreat, and there is growing evidence that this is due to global warming," scientist David Vaughan of the British Antarctic Survey (BAS) told a news conference.

"The peninsula could end up looking like the Alps if the glaciers retreat far enough from the sea," he said. . . .

Scientists have noted before the shrinkage and breakup of some of Antarctica's giant sea ice shelves, but the new study is the first comprehensive look over a long period at the state of the glaciers that flow into the sea.

Scientists have predicted that global temperatures could rise by up to two degrees centigrade this century, pushing the planet into the unknown with rising sea levels and an increase in extreme weather events threatening millions of lives.

Projections see the Arctic icecap continuing to diminish and eventually disappear in the summer. Governments of the circumpolar north have begun positioning themselves strategically to claim sovereign control over new shipping lanes opened up by the disappearing ice. In an ironic twist, a Reuters news story in 2004 headlined as follows: "Denmark Seeks to Claim North Pole, Hopes to Strike Oil."

Another area of ongoing climate change impact is in the North American West, where tens of millions of acres of forest are being devastated by bark beetles and other infestations. The pests, which have attacked pine, fir, and spruce trees in the U.S. West, British Columbia, and Alaska, are normally contained by severe winters. The warming and mild winters in the region have increased their reproduction, abundance, and geographic range.

Hurricane Katrina, which led to the devastating flooding of New Orleans in 2005, was fueled by the warm waters of the Gulf of Mexico. Global warming has contributed to the warming of the tropical Atlantic, and the number of category 4 and 5 hurricanes—the most severe—has increased sharply in recent decades. One cannot associate a particular hurricane with global warming, but scientists are now reasonably confident that global warming is increasing the odds of intense, high-energy hurricanes.

SOUNDINGS • *The Washington Post*

U.S. PRESSURE WEAKENS G-8 CLIMATE PLAN

WASHINGTON D.C., JUNE 17, 2005—Bush administration officials working behind the scenes have succeeded in weakening key sections of a proposal for joint action by the eight major industrialized nations to curb climate change.

Under U.S. pressure, negotiators in the past month have agreed to delete language that would detail how rising temperatures are affecting the globe, set ambitious targets to cut carbon dioxide emissions and set stricter environmental standards for World Bank–funded power projects, according to documents obtained by The Washington Post. Negotiators met this week in London to work out details of the document, which is slated to be adopted next month at the Group of Eight's annual meeting in Scotland.

The administration's push to alter the G-8's plan on global warming marks its latest effort to edit scientific or policy documents to accord with its position that mandatory carbon dioxide cuts are unnecessary. Under mounting international pressure to adopt stricter controls on heat-trapping gas emissions, Bush officials have consistently sought to modify U.S. government and international reports that would endorse a more aggressive approach to mitigating global warming.

Last week, the New York Times reported that a senior White House official had altered government documents to emphasize the uncertainties surrounding the science on global warming. That official, White House Council on Environmental Quality chief of staff Phillip Cooney, left the administration last Friday to take a public relations job with oil giant Exxon Mobil, a leading opponent of mandatory limits on greenhouse gas emissions.

The wording of the international document, titled "Climate Change, Clean Energy and Sustainable Development," will help determine what, if any, action the G-8 countries will take as a group to combat global warming. Every member nation except the United States has pledged to bring its greenhouse gas emissions down to 1990 levels by 2012 as part of the Kyoto Protocol, an international treaty, and British Prime Minister Tony Blair—who currently heads the G-8—is trying to coax the United States into adopting stricter climate controls.

To date, the industrial countries have contributed far more to the buildup of greenhouse gases than the developing countries—the United States alone is responsible for 30 percent—and they have reaped huge economic benefits in the process. The United States emits roughly the same amount of greenhouse gases as 2.6 billion people living in 150 developing nations. Industrial countries account for about 70 percent of carbon dioxide emissions, about 3.3 tons per capita. By contrast, the developing countries emit the rest at only half a ton per capita. Although developing country emissions of greenhouse gases are increasing rapidly, especially in China and elsewhere in Asia, it is doubtful that the developing nations will act to curb their emissions unless the industrial nations—both richer and the source of most of the climate problems we face—validate the seriousness of the issue and demonstrate their commitment to action by taking the first steps.

At the same time, the developing world is more vulnerable to climate change. Its people are more directly dependent on the natural resource base, more exposed to extreme weather events, and less capable economically and technologically to make needed adaptations. The disruption of water supplies or agriculture, the loss of glacial melt water in spring and summer, as well as rising sea levels and other impacts, could easily contribute to social tensions, violent conflicts, humanitarian emergencies, and the creation of ecological refugees. If these North–South differences are not addressed with great care, they could easily emerge as an increasing source of international tension.

Deforestation

It is estimated that about half of the world's temperate and tropical forests have been cleared, mostly for agriculture. A recent study of deforestation indicates that only about 20 percent of Earth's original forests remain in a wild, unmanaged state, and these areas are decreasing. Forest loss has been particularly serious in the tropics, which are home to about two-thirds of our planet's plant and animal species. The tropical forests encompass almost a billion acres of forested land in the area between the Tropics of Cancer and Capricorn. Brazil, Indonesia, and the Democratic Republic of Congo alone contain half of the world's tropical forests, and the rest are scattered throughout Latin America, Africa, and Asia. In recent decades, the rate of tropical forest loss has been about an acre a second. In terms of total forest area globally, these large losses are only very partially offset by increases in forest area in the United States and some other countries.

Tropical forests are particularly sensitive to disturbances. Although they are among the most productive ecosystems in terms of biological productivity, this productivity is deceptive. Most nutrients are in the plant matter itself, not in the soil. Soils in the tropics are notoriously poor. Furthermore, the sheer diversity of species that makes tropical forests so valuable also diminishes their ability to regenerate. In a 1 acre area of forest, one could find literally hundreds of species of plants, but perhaps only a few specimens per species. After deforestation, often the only plants that can survive in the open, nutrient-poor soil are fire-resistant grasses like *Imperata,* which chokes off the growth of the original species and prevents regeneration of a forest canopy.

Today, central governments own almost 80 percent of the remaining intact forests in developing countries. Forest ownership and management by central governments have sometimes resulted in mismanagement, heavy political and economic pressures to allow cutting and inmigration, and widespread corruption, cronyism, and illegal logging. For example, in Vietnam the government nationalized the entire country's forest estate in the 1960s, leading eventually to a rapid increase in forest destruction nationwide as previous local controls and regulations were superceded by state-owned logging companies.

Many countries with high deforestation rates rank high in the international corruption index. Timber concessions in Indonesia, for example, have been awarded to loyal military officers for political reasons, and they have in turn forged partnerships with business groups to exploit their concessions. Around the world, corruption and mismanagement of forests have often gone together. It has been estimated that about three-fourths of Indonesia's timber trade and half of Vietnam's timber cut is illegally felled.

Timber concessions—the right to take trees—have been granted at below market rates and without safeguards or requirements for good management. Government subsidization of projects like road building has further fueled both timber booms and large-scale settlement. Another favorite policy of forest-rich countries is to promote agricultural development and ranching in previously forested areas, sometimes with government subsidies so deep that the enterprises would be essentially uneconomical without them. Cattle ranching in the Amazon is the most well known example in this regard.

These pressures for forest destruction have been both worsened and ameliorated by international factors. International development agencies like the World Bank, though much better today than in 1980, have poured many

SOUNDINGS • Reuters News Service

BRAZIL GREENS QUIT GOVERNMENT OVER AMAZON DESTRUCTION

BRASILIA, MAY 20, 2005—Legislators for Brazil's small Green Party quit the government on Thursday to protest its failure to prevent a near-record rise in destruction of the Amazon rainforest.

The party said Wednesday's government announcement that Amazon deforestation hit its second-highest level last year was the final straw after what it called a string of disastrous environmental policies by President Luiz Inacio Lula da Silva.

"This government represents one of the biggest-ever reversals for Brazilian environmental policy," said Jovino Candido, one of seven Green Party members in the lower House of Deputies who withdrew support from the ruling coalition in Congress. . . .

Lula entered office in 2003 on high hopes he would control use of threatened Amazon areas and balance needs for environmental protection with economic growth. After 28 months in office environmentalists say he has done more to promote dams, roads and farming in the Amazon than halt destruction of the world's largest rainforest, which is home to up to 30 percent of the world's plant and animal species.

Environmentalists have applauded Lula's efforts to create vast Amazon reserves to promote sustainable use of timber and land resources, but they have criticized his inability to enforce environmental laws protecting the vast jungle.

Illegal loggers, land speculators and farmers deforested an area of rainforest larger than the US state of New Jersey between 2003 and 2004. Brazil's soy and beef farmers often move into deforested areas, driven by high global prices and booming demand for their exports.

millions into dams, highways, power development, and transmigration schemes, often to the detriment of forest areas. Critics of globalization charge that economic globalization and the World Trade Organization are magnifying the trend toward expanded logging by encouraging high levels of foreign investment, weaker domestic regulation in the face of international competition, and loss of local community controls. On the other hand, international aid agencies (including the World Bank), conservation groups, and local authorities have cooperated in protecting many areas of unprecedented size and importance.

Land Degradation and Desertification

Today, about a fourth of Earth's terrestrial surface is devoted to crops, orchards, and rangelands for livestock. Arid and semiarid zones constitute a large share of this area. These drylands are a critical source of food and account for about a fifth of the world's food production. About a fourth of the developing world's people—some 1.3 billion in all—live on these dry and other fragile lands. They are not naturally the most productive of agricultural lands, though irrigation can make a remarkable difference, and they are among the most ecologically vulnerable.

Land degradation when most serious is often called desertification. Desertification is sometimes thought of as spreading sand dunes, and though that is a modest part of the problem, the concept of desertification in use today is much broader. It refers to the impoverishment of ecosystems and productive capacity in drylands and has many symptoms:

- Desolation of native vegetation and landscape devegetation

- Salinization of topsoil and water

- Reduction of surface waters and declining groundwater tables

- Unnaturally high soil erosion

An estimated 80 percent of agricultural land in dry regions suffers from moderate to severe desertification. Africa, which is 70 percent dryland areas, is particularly affected, but so are large areas in India and elsewhere in Asia, as well as major regions of the Western Hemisphere, including the southwestern United States and northern Mexico. Among desertification's many consequences are huge losses in food production, greater vulnerability to drought and famine, ecological refugees, loss of biodiversity, and social unrest.

Desertification is typically caused by overcultivation, overgrazing, and poor irrigation practices. But behind these immediate pressures are deeper factors such as population growth, poverty and lack of alternative livelihoods, concentrated patterns of landownership and control, and large-scale movements of people stemming from the vulnerability of many developing country populations to natural disasters and economic turmoil. Not all the contributing factors are domestic. Desertification's immediate causes are often reinforced by international circumstances. The developing world's agricultural producers lose about US$24 billion a year due to industrial

SOUNDINGS • Reuters News Service

SCARCE, DEGRADED LAND IS SPARK FOR AFRICA CONFLICT

JOHANNESBURG, JULY 26, 2005—On a continent where a man's worth is often measured by his cattle, rivalry for the beasts and the degraded land they graze on is sparking lethal conflicts across Africa.

Observers say the violence is rooted in increasingly parched soil which has been battered by overgrazing, erosion, population growth and global warming, exacerbating struggles among human communities with ancient and blood-stained histories.

Last week cattle rustlers in northern Kenya massacred dozens of villagers, sparking brutal reprisals in a lawless region near the Ethiopian border. The death toll from the mayhem was 80.

Those clashes were the most recent in a cycle of clan killings between herders in Kenya over land and scarce water in the arid north.

On the other side of the continent in mostly desert Niger, nomadic herdsmen and crop farmers are locked in age-old battles.

Explosive population growth has increased pressure on land, forcing farmers to sow crops on "corridors" traditionally used by migrating herders for access to rivers, further stoking conflict.

"This is the age-old farmer/herder conflict, the old Biblical tale of Cain and Abel. The struggle over resources is between people who are using them in different ways," said Henri Josserand, the head of the Food and Agriculture Organization's Global Information and Early Warning System.

country trade barriers and subsidies, indirectly pushing many agriculturalists into marginal lands to make a living.

Freshwater Degradation and Shortages

It is doubtful that any natural areas have been as degraded by human activities as freshwater systems. Natural water courses and the vibrant life associated with them have been extensively affected by dams, dikes, diversions, stream channelization, wetland filling, and other modifications, not to mention pollution. Sixty percent of the world's major river basins have been severely or moderately fragmented by dams or other construction. Much of this activity is done to secure access to the water, but power production, flood control, navigation, and land reclamation have also been important factors. As freshwater is diverted away from natural sources, other ecosystems dependent on that water suffer, such as aquatic systems, wetlands, and forests. Human demand for water climbed ninefold in the twentieth century, much faster than population growth, and the trend continues today. It has been estimated that demands for irrigation and other water needs now claim 20 percent of the world's river supply and that the portion will grow to 40 percent by 2020.

Yet water shortages are already apparent in many countries. Rising demands for water have meant that many rivers no longer reach the sea in the dry season, such as the Colorado, Yellow, Ganges, and Nile, and the Syr Darya and Amu Darya rivers in central Asia. Adding insult to injury, natural watercourses have been the recipients of truly enormous volumes of pollutants around the world, from raw sewage to manufacturing effluents to agricultural and urban runoff to waste heat.

Meeting the world's demands for freshwater is proving problematic. About a third of the world's people already live in countries that are classified as "water stressed," meaning that already 20 to 40 percent of the available freshwater is being used by human societies. Projections indicate that the number of such people could rise from about 40 percent to 65 percent by 2025. About a billion people, a fifth of the world's population, lack clean drinking water; 40 percent lack sanitary services. According to WHO calculations, each year about 5 million people die from diseases caused by un-

---

SOUNDINGS • *Wall Street Journal*

WATER SECTOR RIDES A WAVE OF STRONG DEMAND

APRIL 15, 2005—Exploding global demand for water for drinking, agriculture and industry is creating a business boom for companies involved in the delivery, purification, storage and other aspects of H_2O. That is prompting a slew of corporations—including General Electric Co., ITT Industries Inc., Siemens AG, Tyco International Ltd. and Danaher Corp.—to invest billions of dollars in water-related endeavors that are beginning to produce a wave of profits.

The surge in interest in the $400 billion-a-year global business comes as concern grows about the need to upgrade water resources to handle growing populations, give more people access to clean water and deal with a rapidly aging water infrastructure. Demand is growing so quickly that companies dipping their toes into water businesses say these operations are among their fastest-growing units.

safe drinking water and lack of water for sanitation and hygiene. In the poorest countries dehydration and diarrhea are among the most common causes of infant mortality.

The most serious consequences of these freshwater problems are widespread poor health, constrained development of industry and agriculture, loss of services provided by natural aquatic ecosystems (including freshwater fisheries and natural flood control and water purification), species loss, and pollution of coastal areas. Absent a major response, these problems are only expected to increase in coming years.

Freshwater systems become matters of international concern for many reasons. Countries share over 200 river basins around the world, and many of the world's great rivers are shared by five or more countries, including the Amazon, Nile, and Mekong. Resolving international disputes over freshwater has long been a focus of international law and promises to be one of the major international issues of the future. Freshwater is also becoming a commodity in national and international trade as supplies decrease in many parts of the globe. Furthermore, safe water and sanitation have increasingly become focal points for international development cooperation. The United Nations' 2003 *World Water Development Report* concludes that 25 years of international conferences have thus far generated only modest action on freshwater problems. The report notes that to meet internationally agreed water supply and sanitation targets, 342,000 additional people will have to be provided with sanitation every day until 2015.[10]

Marine Fisheries Decline

It is difficult to exaggerate the negative impact that human societies are having on the health of marine fisheries. In 1960, 5 percent of marine fisheries were fished to capacity or overfished. Today that number is 75 percent. The global catch of fish has gone down steadily since 1988 (once the highly volatile Peruvian anchoveta catch is out of the calculation). In 2003, scientists reported that populations of large predator fish—including popularly consumed varieties such as swordfish, marlin, and tuna—are down 90 percent over original stocks; only 10 percent remain. Over 300,000 whales, dolphins, and other cetaceans die each year from entanglement in nets and other fishing gear. Each year 44 billion pounds of fish—about a quarter of the total landed weight—is discarded as unwanted bycatch.

Overfishing is the key culprit here, but the marine environment is also being affected by destruction of mangroves and coastal wetlands, about half

---

SOUNDINGS • *New York Times*

SCIENTISTS WARN FEWER KINDS OF FISH ARE SWIMMING THE OCEANS

JULY 29, 2005—Researchers who studied decades of catch records from Japanese fishing fleets say fishing has greatly reduced the diversity of fish in the world's open oceans, leaving ocean ecosystems less resilient against environmental changes like global warming.

The scientists, who report their findings in today's issue of the journal Science, say it has been known for some time that fishing has reduced species diversity in coastal areas. But they say their study is the first broad look at diversity across open oceans.

The Japanese data records the catches in 50 years of fishing for 15 species of tuna and billfish like marlin and swordfish. But the researchers cross-referenced this information with data collected about more than 140 species by American and Australian government agencies in the 1990's, and the results suggest their conclusions apply more widely. Boris Worm, a biologist at Dalhousie University, in Nova Scotia and a lead author of the paper, said, "The oceans have been drained of species, basically." He said that more must be done to protect areas where diversity persists. . . . .

In many areas, the researchers say, species diversity has fallen by half since the 1950's, meaning that boats now typically catch half the number of tuna and billfish species they did then.

---

of which have been lost, and by pollution and silt from runoff. Particularly hard hit have been the coral reefs. About 20 percent of coral reefs worldwide have been lost, and a further 20 percent are severely threatened.

Beyond biodiversity loss, there are major consequences for human societies stemming from the depletion of the oceans. In Asia, fish are the principal protein source for about half the population. A fifth of the world's people get a fifth or more of their protein from fish. Fishery exports are an important economic asset for developing countries; they are responsible for half the world's export of fish. Indirectly fish products serve as a major source of fertilizer and nutrient for commercial livestock.

Many factors contribute to overfishing. A major cause has been the efforts of some maritime countries, including the United States and Japan, to subsidize their fishing industries. In addition, many migratory species of fish are caught in the open oceans—outside the national sovereignty of any particular country. In such areas no country is able to enforce limits on fisheries takings, nor do many countries feel the responsibility for formulating policies for such areas beyond national control.

Toxic Pollutants

Among the most serious environmental threats to human health and to ecosystems are chemicals known as persistent organic pollutants, or POPs. Rachel Carson's book *Silent Spring,* published in 1962, highlighted for a wide audience the dangers of these new manufactured chemical compounds, such as the then commonly used pesticide DDT. "For the first time in the history of the world, every human being is now subjected to contact with dangerous chemicals, from the moment of conception until death. In the less than two decades of their use, the synthetic pesticides have been so thoroughly distributed throughout the animate and inanimate world that they occur virtually everywhere."[11]

In particular, DDT was driving many species toward extinction, including such formerly common birds as the peregrine falcon, the bald eagle, and the brown pelican. Carson's book ignited environmental litigation that led to the banning of DDT, aldrin-dieldrin, and several other pesticides in the 1970s.

Many of the substances Carson first brought to attention were persistent and not easily biodegradable; as a result, they remain in human and animal systems and can build up, or bioaccumulate, to harmful levels in the fatty tissues of living organisms. Certain POPs can cause cancer and birth defects as well as interfere with hormonal and immune system functioning.

Child health experts at Mount Sinai School of Medicine in New York report that today virtually every person on Earth can be shown to harbor detectible levels of dozens of POPs. It has been known for a long time that POPs were showing up all over the globe, even far outside the range of where the POPs were originally used. For example, Inuit mothers in the Arctic have been measured to have levels of POPs in their breast milk five times greater than found in industrial countries.

One important subcategory of POPs are known as endocrine disrupting substances (EDSs). Many of them can disrupt natural hormone functioning in humans, leading to feminization, low sperm count, and hermaphroditism. While acknowledging that large uncertainties remain in our knowledge of these EDSs, the Mount Sinai School of Medicine researchers believe that "enough evidence has accumulated to justify moving aggressively to limit environmental dispersion of endocrine disruptors."[12]

SOUNDINGS • *Los Angeles Times*

STUDY FINDS GENITAL ABNORMALITIES IN BOYS

MAY 27, 2005—Scientists studying the effects of hormone-mimicking chemicals on humans have reported that compounds called phthalates, used in plastics and beauty products and widely found in people, seem to alter the reproductive organs of baby boys.

In the first study of humans exposed in the womb to phthalates, the researchers, who examined the genitalia of male babies and toddlers, found a strong relationship between the chemicals and subtle changes in the size and anatomy of the children's genitals. Phthalates are ubiquitous compounds used as softeners in plastics and to maintain color and fragrance in beauty products such as nail polish and perfume, among other uses.

It is the first time that scientists have shown that any industrial compound measured in mothers' bodies seems to disrupt the reproductive systems of their babies.

But many experts, including the authors of the report published today in the online version of the journal Environmental Health Perspectives, say that more research must be done to determine if the genital abnormalities in the boys lead to fertility or health problems and to prove that they are caused by phthalates.

The findings were based on tests of 85 mothers and sons, averaging nearly 13 months of age, born in Los Angeles, Minneapolis and Columbia, Mo. Mothers with the highest levels of chemicals in their urine late in their pregnancies had babies with a cluster of effects. The span between anus and penis, called anogenital distance, was comparatively short, and the infants had smaller penises and scrotums and more instances of incomplete descent of testicles.

Medical experts do not know whether babies with those physical characteristics will later develop reproductive problems. But in newborn animals, laboratory studies show that that combination of effects can lead to lower sperm counts, infertility, reduced testosterone and testicular abnormalities when they mature.

The long-term human health effect of today's widespread POP exposures remains unclear overall. One reason is that so few chemicals have been thoroughly tested, even at this late date. The U.S. Environmental Protection Agency (EPA) recently reviewed data on about 3,000 synthetic chemicals in commercial use. For over 40 percent, there was a complete absence of toxicity data; full tests were available for only 7 percent.

But the POP issue is only one of many toxic and hazardous substance problems to attract international attention. Inorganic chemicals, notably the heavy metals like mercury, are also receiving international attention as pollutants. An assessment by the U.N. Environment Programme on mercury's threat to humans and wildlife has led to an international plan to help reduce mercury releases, much of which comes from coal-burning power plants. Mercury is a potent neurotoxin, and perhaps a third of mercury deposition in the United States comes from sources outside the country. Though legislation is before the U.S. Congress to reduce mercury emissions, it is doubtful that anything short of international action will suffice. Beyond mercury, a wide range of toxic substances continue to pose environmental threats—hazardous and radioactive wastes and other heavy metals including lead and arsenic among them.

Loss of Biological Diversity

While attention has typically focused on endangered species and their possible extinction, the broader concept of biological diversity, or biodiversity, is more fundamental. Biodiversity is defined as having three dimensions: the genetic variety within a given species; the millions of individual species of plants, animals, and microorganisms; and the diversity of different types of ecosystems such as alpine tundra, southern hardwood bottomlands, or tropical rainforests.

The focus on biodiversity as opposed to individual species was warmly embraced by many in the 1980s and 1990s, and it soon became a dominant paradigm in the biological sciences. New journals, such as *Conservation Biology* and *Biodiversity and Conservation,* sprang up. In the process, the idea of biodiversity has sometimes come to represent the field of conservation and the science of ecology writ large. As E. O. Wilson asserted in his popular book *The Diversity of Life,* "Biological diversity—'biodiversity' in the new parlance—is the key to the maintenance of the world as we know it."[13]

Studies reveal that a large amount of biodiversity is concentrated in a relatively small number of "hotspots." Thirty-four biodiversity hotspots covering about 2.3 percent of Earth's surface, mostly in developing world regions, are home to about two-thirds of the world's species. Species diversity (in terms of numbers per area) generally increases from the poles to the equator, and this pattern has led to biodiversity protection efforts centered heavily in the tropics and, more recently, on the biodiversity hot spots. The generally high species counts in many tropical forests have been one of the main reasons that conservationists have been calling for the protection of these areas for the last 30 years. Scientists estimate that the past loss of about half the tropical forests may have cost us 15 percent of the species in these forests. Destruction of aquatic and wetland habitats has also contributed to serious biodiversity declines.

After habitat loss, the leading cause of species loss is other species, as non-native invasive species have emerged as a huge threat to biodiversity. About 40 percent of the species listed in the United States as endangered or threatened are on the list as a result of threats from invasives. But overharvesting of particular plant and animal species is also a major cause of biodiversity loss, whether we look at codfish, mahogany, or tropical birds. Toxic chemicals, extra ultraviolet radiation, and acidification from acid rain can also contribute to ecosystem impoverishment. Climate change is not yet a major source of biodiversity loss, but many scientists expect it soon to become a major one.

The cumulative effect of all the factors is that species loss today is estimated to be perhaps 1,000 times the natural or normal rate species go extinct. Many scientists believe we are on the brink of the sixth great wave of species loss on Earth, and the only one caused by the human species.

There are many reasons for the world community to be concerned about the loss of biodiversity. One was well stated in the preamble to the 1982

SOUNDINGS • Environmental News Service

ONE IN FOUR BIRD SPECIES COULD DISAPPEAR BY CENTURY'S END

WASHINGTON D.C., DECEMBER 15, 2004—A quarter of the world's bird species will likely be extinct or critically endangered by the end of the century, according to a new study by U.S. researchers.

This projected extinction wave has implications beyond the fate of individual bird species, the researchers said, as the loss of birds will have negative impacts on the environment and may encourage the spread of human disease.

The findings add to growing concern about the planet's biodiversity and echo several other recent studies that indicate conservation efforts are failing.

The most recent Red List of Threatened Species, released late last month by IUCN—The World Conservation Union—indicates that 12 percent of all bird species, 23 percent of all mammal species, one-third of all amphibian species and 42 percent of all turtles and tortoises are already threatened with extinction.

World Charter for Nature: "Every form of life is unique, warranting respect regardless of its worth to man, and to accord other organisms such recognition, man must be guided by a moral code of conduct."[14] In addition to ethical considerations, biodiversity is the source of the ecosystem services that make life possible—ecosystem services such as nutrient cycling, pollination, air and water purification, climate regulation, drought and flood control, not to mention the commercial products of field, forest, and stream. Consider that many oils, chemicals, rubber, spices, nuts, honey, and fruits were first harvested in the wild; moreover, a third of all prescription drugs were originally harvested as substances found in nature. Many nongovernmental organizations (NGOs) have made protection of biodiversity a centerpiece of their land conservation strategies and now often include attention to the economic benefits of biodiversity as a factor in protected areas plans.

Excess Nitrogen

The nine global challenges just discussed were all identified as early as 1980 as major threats meriting international action. The problem of excess nitrogen in ecosystems has not received similar recognition, but it deserves to be on this list of serious threats.

Earth's atmosphere is mostly nitrogen, bound together as N_2 and not reactive. Bacteria such as those associated with legumes "fix" nitrogen, changing it to a biologically active form that plants can use. But here is the problem: we humans have started fixing nitrogen too, industrially. Today humans are fixing as much nitrogen as nature does. Once fixed, nitrogen remains active for a very long time, cascading through the biosphere.

Today, the anthropogenic nitrogen is coming primarily from two sources: about 75 percent from fertilizers and 25 percent from fossil fuel combustion. Nitrogen fertilizers are often ammonia based; their use is a huge global enterprise. Ninety percent of this fertilizer is wasted, though, ending up in waterways and in the air and soil. High-temperature combustion in power plants oxidizes the nitrogen to produce a variety of nitrogen oxides.

Nitrogen in waterways leads to overfertilization and, when heavy, to algal blooms and eutrophication—aquatic life simply dies from lack of oxygen. There are now over 150 dead zones in the oceans, mostly due to excess fertilization. Nitrate in ground and surface waters is also a threat to human health. And there is another pathway. Forty percent of the world's grain goes to feed livestock, which produce vast volumes of nitrogen-rich manure,

---

SOUNDINGS • Nature

NITROGEN STUDY FERTILIZES FEARS OF POLLUTION

FEBRUARY 24, 2005—Urgent political and scientific action is needed to tackle the global threat of nitrogen pollution, say scientists behind one of the field's biggest research projects.

They gathered in London last week to mark the completion of a five-year, £7-million (US $14-million) project to map the effects of excess nitrogen on forests, rivers and grasslands, primarily in Britain.

The researchers say that the Global Nitrogen Enrichment (GANE) programme has transformed their understanding of how nitrogen affects the environment. But a lack of similar studies in other countries has led to inadequate legislation, which is generating a growing threat to global biodiversity, they say. Previous efforts have been made to draw attention to the issue, but researchers say that much more needs to be done.

"This is the third major threat to our planet after biodiversity loss and climate change," says John Lawton, chief executive of the Natural Environment Research Council, which provided the bulk of the funding for GANE. "It's manifestly unsustainable in the long term."

---

much of which ends up in the water. All this extra nitrogen is also having affects on biodiversity and natural systems—shifting the species composition of ecosystems by favoring those that respond most to nitrogen. Absent corrective action, nitrogen added to waterways is projected to increase 25 percent in the Organization for Economic Cooperation and Development (OECD) countries and 100 percent in the developing world between 1995 and 2020.

In the air, nitrogen oxide from fossil fuel combustion reacts with volatile hydrocarbons and sunlight to produce smog, a nasty mix of photochemical oxidants, one of which is ozone. It can also become nitric acid and contribute to acid deposition. Ozone (from smog) and nitrous oxide (from fertilized soils) are greenhouse gases, so nitrogen fixation also contributes to global warming. As the 2001 Summary Statement from the Second International Nitrogen Conference notes, biologically active nitrogen can "contribute to smog, fine particle formation, visibility impairment, acid deposition, excess nutrient inputs to estuaries and near-coastal waters, global warming, and stratospheric ozone depletion."[15] Essential to life and necessary in our gardens and agricultural fields, nitrogen is the classic case of too much of a good thing. The problem is global. Asia now contributes 35 percent of the world's synthetic nitrogen. Serious though this problem is, it has yet to attract the attention that CFCs or carbon dioxide have received.

Some Connections among the Issues

An important observation about the global environmental challenges is that there are complex linkages among them. The previous discussions of biodiversity and excess nitrogen dramatize this point. Because of such connections and interactions, these problems are especially difficult to manage effectively. The interconnections among the issues also bring to the fore a key feature of global policymaking—the management of uncertainty and risk.

Fossil fuel use—the burning of coal, oil, and natural gas—provides one type of linkage. Fossil fuels are responsible for acid rain and most of the human-induced climate change. They also cause the buildup of tropospheric ozone (smog occurring at Earth's surface), which itself is a greenhouse gas in addition to being a health hazard and destroyer of crops and forests, where it often acts in concert with acid rain.

Another set of considerations link climate change and stratospheric ozone depletion. CFCs and certain other gases that deplete the ozone layer are also greenhouse gases, contributing to global warming. (There are also CFC substitutes that are greenhouse gases.) Global warming can actually cool the stratosphere and that in turn can worsen ozone depletion. And the increase in UVB radiation due to the thinner ozone layer can alter Earth's ecosystems and interact with the terrestrial and aquatic effects of climate change.

Deforestation contributes to biodiversity loss, climate change, and desertification. Climate change, acid rain, ozone depletion, toxic chemicals, and water reductions can in turn adversely affect world forests.

Because climate provides the setting or envelope for life, changing climate will affect everything. Among other things, it is likely to worsen desertification, lead to both additional flooding and increased droughts, impact fresh water supplies, adversely affect biodiversity and forests, and further degrade aquatic ecosystems.

It is impossible to isolate environmental issues from economic ones. For instance, industrialization and the growth of world trade have contributed directly to the widespread use of fossil fuels, the global transport of oil by ships, and the broader transportation of goods by ship worldwide. The increased reliance on imported oil increases the likelihood of oil spills. Marine commerce provides the vectors by which alien species invasions occur, as foreign species hitch rides on ships and then enter new ecosystems where there are no natural predators.

Many uncertainties attend these interactive effects and their likely environmental and social consequences. It is difficult to make rational policies for large-scale environmental threats because of the extensive uncertainties that surround them. For instance, decision makers typically lack full information about exact levels of contamination in a particular ecosystem, the capacity of the ecosystem and its species to assimilate some degree of contamination, the effects of contaminants at various levels of concentration, the likely pattern of additional contamination in the future, the interactions among environmental threats, and so on. Further, groups often disagree on the appropriate policy responses to dealing with threats, from preferences for outright bans on environmentally harmful activities, to command and control approaches reflecting a scientific assessment of a particular ecosystem's ability to sustain stress, to economic instruments such as pollution charges.

Vaclav Smil nicely captures this problem for governance: "Confident diagnoses of the state of our environment remain elusive. Even where we have a fairly solid quantitative base, divergent interpretations can stretch the data in the direction of desired policy-making conclusions. These weaknesses are compounded in forecasts. We can simulate accurately many complex physical processes, and we can turn this ability into outstanding technical designs. But even our best simulations of long-term interactions among environmental, economic, technical and social developments have been simplistic and misleading."[16]

Such problems demand new approaches to governance. Many observers have argued that the scope of knowledge necessary to make informed judgment requires opening up the decision-making process to the widest possible array of participants and interest.

Underlying Drivers of Deterioration

The 10 major global environmental challenges can be thought of as the end result of an interacting set of underlying causes, or drivers, of deterioration. Understanding these drivers is important for the simple reason that, in the end, societies will have to come to grips with them to forestall an appalling deterioration of our natural assets.

Three of the more obvious root causes of these problems are conveniently described in what is called the "IPAT equation," which sees environmental impact (I) as the product of population (P), affluence (A), and technology (T). The equation is actually a mathematical identity (Impact = Population × GDP/Population × Impact/GDP), but it usefully links three of the driving forces behind increased environmental consequences. Consider, for example, carbon dioxide emissions as a measure of environmental impact. If population doubles in a given period of time and per capita incomes go up threefold, and nothing else changes, we would expect CO_2 emission to go up sixfold. If they actually went up by only fourfold, it would be because technological change had made it possible to produce each dollar of GDP with less CO_2 emissions. The society in

Three of the more obvious root causes of these problems are conveniently described in what is called the "IPAT equation," which sees environmental impact (I) as the product of population (P), affluence (A), and technology (T).

SOUNDINGS • **Environmental News Service**

U.S. POPULATION PREDICTED TO BOOM BY 2050

WASHINGTON D.C., AUGUST 18, 2004—With 294 million people, the United States is now the world's third most populous country after China and India. According to a new forecast from the Population Reference Bureau, the U.S. population will increase by 45 percent over the next 45 years, the only industrialized nation projected to experience a major population increase.

The total world population will likely reach 9.3 billion by mid-century, up from the 6.3 billion people on Earth today.

The nonprofit Population Reference Bureau based in Washington, issued its annual datasheet on Monday, showing that by 2025, the U.S. population will increase to 349.4 million people, and by 2050 that number will be up to nearly 420 million.

This population increase, made up of a combination of an increasing birth rate and increasing immigration, will result in a population density of 79 people per square mile by 2050, the Population Reference Bureau (PRB) predicts.

This will put pressure on all U.S. natural resources—water, agricultural land, fuel, timber, fisheries—and living space.

question would be decreasing what is called the carbon intensity of production. Carbon intensity, which has in fact been decreasing in the United States, can be cut by increasing energy efficiency, by shifting to nonfossil energy (renewables and nuclear power), and by shifting to the lighter hydrocarbons—oil and natural gas—within the fossil fuel family. These are all different types of technological change within the framework of the IPAT equation.

The fourfold expansion in human numbers in the twentieth century, from 1.5 billion to over 6 billion, has been a huge driver of environmental decline. And the story is far from over. Global population is projected to go up another 25 percent in the next 20 years. Virtually all of the current growth is in the developing world, but this has not always been the case. The billion or so souls in the rich countries had their population explosion earlier, and these countries have now largely completed what is called the demographic transition. The transition begins when improvements in health and nutrition lead to reduced infant mortality and longer lives. Fertility rates do not immediately decline, so population grows rapidly. Later, fertility rates decline and population size tends again toward stability. The transition is thus one from high births and high deaths to low births and low deaths. Indeed, in some industrial countries birth rates are now well below replacement levels.

It is possible that the demographic transition will be completed in the developing world around midcentury and that global population growth may level off at about 9 billion and then perhaps begin to decline. These numbers may be optimistic and depend importantly on continuation of national and international population programs.

The IPAT equation also helps us see a key fact about population growth. In highly affluent societies, a given increase in population numbers will have a disproportionately large environmental impact, based on today's patterns of resource consumption and pollution. As immigration accounted for about a third of U.S. population growth during the 1990s, and U.S. population growth is one of the highest in the world in numbers of people added per year, this consideration has led a few environmentalists to question U.S. immigration policy—a thorny issue, to be sure—and to call for a U.S. population growth policy.

In the developing world today, high fertility rates are often driven by a set of reinforcing factors: the status of women, lack of employment opportunities for women and educational opportunities for girls, lack of maternal and child health care and family planning services, as well as poverty and deprivation generally. Addressing these issues together can lead to dramatic declines in fertility rates.

Affluent lifestyles are a second major driver of deterioration. We live in a consumer society, and, despite some modest efforts at recycling, it is still a throw-away society. If an appliance or gadget goes on the blink, toss it. Take a look at *Wired* magazine, popular with the high-tech set where one might hope to find a new lifestyle emerging. There, among the expected ads for software and hardware, one finds ads for elegant muscle cars, mega-HDTV setups, designer coffees and vodkas, fancy hotels, camcorders and other electronic devices, credit cards, and so on.

The consumption habits of the affluent have been repeatedly cited both for their environmental impacts and for their assault on equity: "We are all consuming more on a per capita basis in the U.S., Europe, and Asia, resulting in accelerated use of natural resources and associated environmental impacts both at home and abroad. Indeed, more goods and services have been consumed since 1950 than by all previous generations combined. From 1950 to 1990, per capita consumption of copper, steel, energy, timber and meat doubled; consumption of plastic increased five-fold and aluminum by seven-fold. While America has the highest per capita consumption levels in the world, the resource consumption in Western Europe and Japan is only slightly less. . . .

"Consumption raises troubling equity issues. Until the mid-18th century, improvements in living standards worldwide were barely perceptible. Most societies were resigned to poverty as an inescapable fact of life. Since 1950 the richest 20% of humankind has doubled its per-capita consumption of energy, meat, timber, steel, and copper, and quadrupled its car ownership, greatly increasing global emissions of CFCs and greenhouse gases, accelerating topical deforestation, and intensifying other environmental impacts. In 1999, people living in the world's richest 20% of countries consumed 86% of the world's GNP."[17]

The third IPAT factor, technology, is at least as important as the other two. Indeed if one assumes that population and affluence will generally increase for the foreseeable future, only rapid changes in technology—the greening of technology—offers hope within IPAT for reducing environmental impacts. Of the three, it's the only term that promises movement in the "right" direction. We saw this important reality in the IPAT example involving CO_2 emissions and carbon intensity.

The core problem in this context is that most of the technologies (including techniques) that today dominate agriculture, energy, manufacturing, transportation, and the built environment were developed in an era when environmental considerations, far from being dominant ones, were hardly considerations at all.

The situation regarding technology is thus much like that on consumption. Public attitudes toward new technology have generally been supportive, welcoming, and trustful. (This receptivity is still causing us to overlook possible impacts of information technology, robotics, nanotechnologies, and genetic engineering.) The control of technologies has been largely in the hands of large corporations that benefit from their deployment and are clearly in no position to be impartial judges of the public's best interests. The unaided market fails to guide technology toward good environmental choices; governments have failed to correct poor market signals. And once a technology has reached a certain level of deployment, it gains an often unwelcome lifespan.

At a deeper level, beyond the immediate drivers reflected in the IPAT equation, we find a variety of other drivers at work. Several involve the nature of our economic system: a deep commitment to continuing high rates of economic growth—what has been called "growthmania" or "the growth fetish"; the concentration of power in a relatively small number of large corporations and the narrow imperatives of profitability that impel their operations; a market economy guided by prices and other market signals that are environmentally misleading because they do not incorporate the full environmental costs of doing business (an example of "market failure"); and an ongoing economic globalization that is largely unregulated for environmental and social ends and thus is an accelerator of all these forces because it speeds patterns of growth and development that remain unsustainable environmentally.

> *Several drivers involve the nature of our economic system: a deep commitment to continuing high rates of economic growth—what has been called "growthmania" or "the growth fetish."*

An additional driver, the opposite of affluence, is world poverty and the extreme gaps in incomes between poor and rich countries. The conventional observation that the poor are often forced to degrade their own environments because no alternatives are open to them is still valid in a world where at least a billion people

Growth At All Costs

Many neoclassical economists have cited higher levels of economic growth as a potential solution for environmental threats. The argument is that economic progress tends to correlate with increasing environmental protection. In other words, societies can grow out of their problems. However, some, such as historian J. R. McNeill, argue that the obsession with economic growth has been enormously destructive. "The growth fetish, while on balance quite useful in a world with empty land, shoals of undisturbed fish, vast forests, and a robust ozone shield, helped create a more crowded and stressed one. Despite the disappearance of ecological buffers and mounting real costs, ideological lock-in reigned in both capitalist and communist circles. No reputable sect amongst economists could account for depreciating natural assets. The true heretics, economists who challenged the fundamental goal of growth and sought to recognize value in ecosystem services, remained outside the pale to the end of the century. Economic thought did not adjust to the changed conditions it helped create; thereby it continued to legitimate, and indeed indirectly cause, massive and rapid ecological change. The overarching priority of economic growth was easily the most important idea of the twentieth century."*

*McNeill, J. R. 2000. *Something New under the Sun: An Environmental History of the Twentieth-Century World.* New York: W. W. Norton, 336.

live in conditions of abject poverty and extreme deprivation and where close to half the world's people survive on less than $2 per day. The search for land pushes them into forest; the need for fuelwood and structural material leads to denuding the landscape; the imperative of supplying food leads to excessive cropping and grazing. Meanwhile, the absolute and the relative poverty of the majority of nations creates a powerful push for economic growth at all costs, including environmental ones. Per capita GDP of the United States in 2002 was $36,000; in Europe, $22,900; in China, $980; in India, $490; and in Nigeria, $360 or about $1 per day per person.

Beyond all these factors, at the deepest level there are systems of values and habits of thought that conspire against environmental protection. Two ingrained ones in our society go by the awkward words *anthropocentrism* and *contempocentrism*. The former puts humans at the center of the world often at the expense of other life on Earth. In the process it ignores one of the two guiding principles of environmental ethics: our duty to the community

Aldo Leopold and Preston Cloud: Environmental Ethics

Aldo Leopold was an American ecologist and forester whose posthumously published collection of essays, *A Sand County Almanac*, is considered a groundbreaking text on conservation. In the essays, Leopold outlines the concept of a land ethic that requires humans to reassess their relationship with the environment: "A land ethic changes the role of *Homo sapiens* from conqueror of the land-community to plain member and citizen of it. . . . Quit thinking about decent land-use as solely an economic problem. Examine each question in terms of what is ethically and esthetically right, as well as what is economically expedient. A thing is right when it tends to preserve the integrity, stability, and beauty of the biotic community. It is wrong when it tends otherwise."*

Leopold believed that we have obligations to nature "over and above those dictated by self-interest." If we humans have rights, nature does also. The life that evolved here with us should be allowed to live "as a matter of biotic right."

Just as Leopold wrote eloquently about our duties to other life on the landscape, Preston Cloud, the far-sighted biogeologist who wrote *Cosmos, Earth and Man* in 1978, forcefully addressed our duties to future generations: "Who then will speak for posterity in today's world? The industrialized regions of the world react primarily to market pressures, while the theory of competitive markets, in addition to excluding community assets such as air, water, and scenery, assumes all participants to be fully informed and free to choose. But posterity cannot participate in its own behalf. It has no information and no choice—not even the choice to go unborn. There is no term for it in the economic equation. The third world, for its part, must struggle too hard to shelter and feed itself to think in the long term. We are prone to dodge the issue of posterity's rights with the complacent judgment that, after all, no one can foresee the future, and that each generation must therefore look after its own needs as they come along, with whatever means avail. "There is some truth to that view, but more escapism. . . . We are not mere pawns of fate. We can to some degree foresee the consequences of our actions and take heed not only for our own welfare in years to come but also in the interests of future generations. All our yesterdays need not have passed in vain. Our knowledge of past events, current trends, biological and societal processes, and natural laws can be brought to bear in attempts to anticipate

continued

continued

the future and to exercisesome control over it. From such considerations arises a responsibility to posterity that cannot be set aside merely because we cannot see exactly how to fulfill it in all particulars."***

*Leopold, A. 1949. *A Sand County Almanac.* London: Oxford University Press, 204, 211.

**Cloud, P. 1978. *Cosmos, Earth and Man.* New Haven: Yale University Press, 302–304.

of life that evolved here with us. The
latter—contempocentrism—dis-
counts the future in favor of the present and thus violates the other key
principle of environmental ethics—
our duty to future generations.

> **Contempocentrism** *discounts the future in favor of the present and thus violates the other key principle of environmental ethics—our duty to future generations.*

The need to address these deeper,
underlying forces contributing to de-
terioration of the global environment is a principal theme of chapter 6.

From Stockholm to Johannesburg: First Attempt at Global Environmental Governance

IN OUR THOUGHT EXPERIMENT IN CHAPTER I, WE CONSIDERED THE PROSPECT of governing and managing the settlement of our 6.5 billion fellow travelers on a pristine Earth, guided by a strict concept of sustainable development. We noted the difficulty of that challenge and then observed that it would be child's play compared with the actual challenge we face of managing a transition to sustainability in the real world we have inherited. Now that we have confronted the major global environmental threats in chapter 2 and examined the powerful forces behind those threats, it is easy to see why this is so. Many communities of intellectuals, activists, and managers believe that "their" issues are the most important ones, and perhaps we, as authors, are similarly biased, but it is hard not to conclude that the stakes involved in addressing the challenges sketched in the preceding chapter are among the very highest human societies have ever faced.

Despite the daunting list of challenges, the news is not all bad. As we shall see in this chapter, starting in the 1980s governments and others did begin the quest for planetary stewardship. It is important to acknowledge what has been accomplished. An "agenda" of the principal large-scale environmental concerns was forcefully identified for governmental action. In response to this agenda, there has been an upsurge of international conferences, negotiations, action plans, treaties, and other initiatives. New fields of international environmental law and diplomacy have been born. There has been a vast outpouring of impressive and relevant scientific research and policy analysis. In academia, international environmental affairs has become a major subject of intellectual inquiry and teaching.

An ever-stronger international community of environmental and conservation groups has flourished. Both national governments and multilateral institutions, from the United Nations to the international development banks, have recognized these concerns, creating major units to address global environmental issues. Many multinational corporations have become highly innovative and have moved ahead with impressive steps, often before their governments have.

How did the global environmental agenda emerge in the first place? How were the issues identified and framed? How did various actors gain recognition and political traction? How did events unfold, and which are the more important developments? What has been accomplished to date in the area of global environmental governance? This chapter takes up these questions by reviewing the history of the last few decades, using as milestones the major global conferences on the environment.

The first of these, the 1972 Stockholm conference on the Human Environment, was followed by others, notably the UN Conference on Environment and Development held in Rio de Janeiro in 1992 (otherwise known as the Earth Summit) and the World Summit on Sustainable Development held in Johannesburg in 2002. These gatherings of governments, nongovernmental organizations (NGOs), business leaders, the media, and others provide useful points of reference to follow the unfolding responses to the global agenda.

*The first of these, the 1972 Stockholm conference on the Human Environment, was followed by others, notably the **UN Conference on Environment and Development held in Rio de Janeiro in 1992** (otherwise known as the **Earth Summit**) and the World Summit on Sustainable Development held in Johannesburg in 2002.*

Before taking up this history, we should ask an important question: Once governments and others were faced with the need to respond to the global environmental threats reviewed in chapter 2, what options were open to them?

There are two broad areas of possible response:

- Governmental responses, in which governments use their powers to tax, spend, and regulate to address the challenges. Within the broad arena of governmental response, there are two major subareas:

unilateral action and multilateral action (i.e., action taken in concert with other nations);

- Private, voluntary responses in which corporations and consumers see it is in their own long-term best interest, for example, to forgo the use of ozone-depleting substances or the purchase of wood products from biodiversity hot spots around the world.

*Within the broad arena of governmental response, there are two major subareas: **unilateral action and multilateral action** (i.e., action taken in concert with other nations)*

Possibly, there are situations where private, voluntary responses might be largely sufficient to contain an emerging environmental threat. As a result of public and consumer pressure as well as internal corporate leadership, Home Depot and Unilever took decisions to give priority in their purchases to forest and fish products that are produced under rigorous sustainability criteria. These forest and fishery certification processes have evolved outside of government. These initiatives have not solved the underlying problems of deforestation and fisheries depletion, to say the least, but they do underscore that voluntary actions can be important if they become the rule and not the exception.

One can also imagine situations where unilateral actions by individual governments—actions taken domestically, perhaps without much coordination with other governments—prove important in addressing a global challenge. As we saw in chapter 2, emissions of ozone-depleting chlorofluorocarbons (CFCs) declined in the late 1970s as the result of individual consumer decisions and unilateral national actions in the United States and elsewhere to stop some uses of these chemicals, especially their use as propellants in aerosol cans.

That said, the CFC case is also a leading example of the limitations of both voluntary and unilateral approaches. After declining in the 1970s, CFC use began climbing again in the 1980s, sparking new international concern and demands for additional action. Consumer decisions were proving incapable of addressing all the uses of CFCs, and nations were unwilling to unilaterally jeopardize their national industries by tighter domestic regulation. The process of controlling CFC use thus turned inevitably to building a multilateral regulatory system where issues of equity among countries and timetables for phasing out CFC use could be negotiated and then resolved by all the countries with a stake in the outcome, as we explore in more detail in chapter 4.

There are several reasons why governments, even those with the best of intentions, typically cannot address global environmental problems with unilateral action. Governments will rarely act in a way that puts their economies and their companies at a competitive disadvantage. There is also the problem of futility: often the challenge cannot be met by one country or even a small group of countries acting alone, and broader participation is a prerequisite for success. Finally, there are those situations where the source of the problem is beyond the country's boundaries.

For all these reasons, multilateral cooperation is almost always essential in addressing serious global environmental challenges. Yet the multilateral approach still leaves open several options for governments to:

- agree informally on what must be done and then each separately do it;

- agree formally on what must be done but capture that agreement in a nonbinding, "soft law" text; or

- enter into a formal treaty agreement, a binding accord with the force of law—"hard law" (often referred to as a "multilateral environmental agreement" or MEA).

In each of these three cases, the intergovernmental accord can address how best to use governments' powers to tax, spend, and regulate. A multilateral agreement, for example, might be essentially regulatory, such as banning certain persistent organic pollutants such as DDT and polychlorinated biphenyl (PCB). Or it might be an

Enter into a formal treaty agreement, a binding accord with the force of law—"hard law" (often referred to as a "multilateral environmental agreement" or MEA)

agreement on the policies needed to realize sustainable development in a particular sector of the economy. Or it might be an agreement on how to increase development assistance spending on environmental and resource objectives.

Just as there are pressures that push toward multilateral cooperation, there are also pressures that push multilateral cooperation toward the third option—binding treaties, or MEAs. If an agreement is not binding on the parties, there is a greater risk that it will not be taken seriously. Only when an agreement is binding will the parties be sufficiently engaged to work out an agreement that they truly accept and intend to implement. If you are really serious, or you want the world to think you are, you write a law. When you write a law bilaterally or multilaterally, you have a treaty. The treaty can be between two countries (like the U.S.–Canada acid rain agreement), or regional (like the European acid rain agreement), or global (like the treaties on climate change and biological diversity).

Likewise, there are pressures that push toward regulatory-type approaches in treaty writing. Mandated goals with quantitative targets and timetables can be more easily monitored and are good at forcing action. Most governments seek to control the size of their budgets and to contain public spending. Regulation is cheaper than spending, for governments in any case. Moreover, regulatory (and tax) approaches can support the policy of making the polluter or resource users pay for environmental cleanup or for the environmental damage they cause.

Within this broad framework, let us now examine the actual response to global environmental concerns that unfolded in the journey from the Stockholm conference in 1972 through the Johannesburg summit in 2002. As we shall see, governments have in fact relied heavily on formal treaties in addressing global environmental challenges. Other avenues have been pursued, such as somewhat increased government spending on these issues, but the primary focus of the international community has been on the development of international environmental law, principally treaties (conventions and protocols) but also including soft law, the nonbinding international policy declarations. The principal feature of the international community's first attempt at global environmental governance has been the rapid development of international environmental law. Much less attention has been given to creating the conditions for success of international environmental law and even less to addressing directly the underlying causes or drivers of global environmental challenges.

The Stockholm Conference: Setting Out

Held in Stockholm, Sweden, the 1972 United Nations Conference on the Human Environment (UNCHE) was the first concerted effort of the international community to focus on the environment as a major topic of international concern and attention. The Stockholm conference was the product of a number of factors, but it is best seen as the international ex-

pression of the huge surge of environmental concern then occurring at the
national level, especially in key industrial countries.

In America, the post–World War II
economic boom gave people greater
leisure time, and outdoor recreation
became popular. National park visita-
tion doubled between 1954 and 1962
and doubled again by 1971. By 1970

*The **Stockholm conference**
was the product of a number of
factors, but it is best seen as
the international expression of
the huge surge of environmental
concern then occurring at the
national level, especially in key
industrial countries.*

there were more Americans in the suburbs than in cities or rural areas.
Yet economic growth had also brought major environmental deterioration. Air and water pollution surged after World War II. Threats were highly
visible and impossible to ignore: smog, soot, and the resultant smarting eyes
and cough from air pollution; streams and beaches closed to fishing and
swimming because of water contaminants; plastic trash and toxic chemicals that would not go away; birds threatened by DDT; pesticide poisoning;
fish kills; power plants and highways in the neighborhood; marshes filled for
new tract houses, and streams channelized for navigation and drainage; clear-
cutting and strip-mining.

There was also a widespread view that major corporations were responsible. Eloquent writers emerged to make the case: Rachel Carson published
Silent Spring in 1962; Ralph Nader wrote *Unsafe at Any Speed* in 1965. The
play had to have a villain, and corporate America was it.

Finally, there were the major precipitating events: the Cuyahoga River
in Cleveland bursting into flames, the Interior Department's proposal to
flood the Grand Canyon, and, most significantly, the Santa Barbara oil spill
in 1969.

Simultaneously, the *Apollo 8* mission to the moon in 1968 made possible a view of Earth from space. The picture of our small blue planet, float-
ing in a seemingly endless void, changed perceptions. The first Earth Day in
1970 launched the new era of environmental concern in the United States.
Concern was not limited to the United States by any means. Similar movements emerged in Canada, Japan, the Nordic countries, and elsewhere.

The broader international political context was also changing in the
1960s. New countries, especially in Asia, Africa, and Latin America, were
emerging as independent entities unshackled from colonialism. Acutely
aware of their histories of colonial economic exploitation, these countries

were anxious about preserving their sovereignty and demonstrating control over their own governance and resources. Poverty, lower life expectancies, illiteracy, lack of basic health amenities, and high population growth rates meant that national priorities in these countries were firmly oriented toward economic and social objectives. The global "South," as these nations came to be known, considered their development priorities to be imperative; they wanted to "catch up" with the richer nations. They also asserted that the responsibility of protecting the environment was primarily on the shoulders of the richer "Northern" nations, who were the big polluters in the first place. Indeed, it was Sweden that initiated the original call for an international conference on the environment. Six months before the Stockholm conference, developing countries passed a UN General Assembly resolution stressing that escalating concerns for the environment should not undermine their economic objectives.

This interplay of environment and development concerns provided the backdrop to the Stockholm conference. The UN General Assembly directed that the conference provide guidelines for action by governments and international organizations to protect and improve the environment. It also highlighted the need to forestall environmental problems in developing countries.

> The global **"South,"** as these nations came to be known, considered their development priorities to be imperative; they wanted to "catch up" with the richer nations. They also asserted that the responsibility of protecting the environment was primarily on the shoulders of the richer **"Northern"** nations, who were the big polluters in the first place.

In preparing for the conference, the developing countries had their first opportunity to formulate their international environmental agenda. The Group of 77—the bargaining bloc within which the developing countries have coordinated their positions at the United Nations— stressed an agenda that highlighted issues of poverty and economic development. This theme was forcefully articulated at Stockholm itself by India's prime minister Indira Gandhi: "Are not poverty and need the greatest polluters? . . . How can we speak to those who live in villages and slums about keeping the oceans, rivers and the air clean when their own lives are contaminated at the source? The environment cannot be improved in conditions of poverty."[1]

The stage was thus set for the longest-running tug-of-war in international environmental politics: North vs. South, environment vs. development, the pollution of the affluent vs. the degradation of poverty. The ongoing struggle to bridge this divide had its first engagement in the little town of Founex, near Geneva. Discussions there among representatives from both industrial and developing countries gave rise to the possibility of a North–South bargain on the environment. This compromise took the form of the doctrine of environment and development—the forerunner to the current mantra of sustainable development—in which governments agreed (1) that environment and development are two mutually reinforcing sides of the same coin, and (2) that the industrial world would accept the principle of "additionality" by which they would pay some or all of the additional costs of environmental initiatives in the developing world with new and additional development assistance resources.

Altogether, 114 government representatives met at Stockholm and debated the environment and development issues of the day. The dominant concerns of countries both North and South were domestic. One hundred thirty-four NGOs participated in unofficial meetings (or "parallel events"), and the presence of journalists and other media made the event a tangible symbol of emerging environmental awareness.

The conference produced considerable results. The most important of these was the Stockholm Declaration, a list of 26 principles highlighting a new ethic intended to govern future behavior of societies toward the environment. The preamble of the declaration called for "a common outlook and principles to inspire and guide the peoples of the world in the preservation and enhancement of the human environment." Principle 1 stated that there was a "fundamental right to freedom, dignity and adequate conditions of life, in an environment of quality" and that all had a "solemn responsibility to protect and improve the environment for present and future generations." Principle 21 affirmed the "sovereign right" of states to exploit resources pursuant to their

> Governments agreed (1) that environment and development are two mutually reinforcing sides of the same coin, and (2) that the industrial world would accept the principle of **"additionality"** by which they would pay some or all of the additional costs of environmental initiatives in the developing world with new and additional development assistance resources.

own environmental policies, but it also proclaimed "the responsibility [of states] to ensure that activities within their jurisdiction or control do not cause damage to the environment of other states." Principle 22 called upon states to cooperate in developing international environmental law on liability and compensation for the international environmental consequences of domestic actions.[2]

Another important output was the *Stockholm Action Plan,* a set of 109 policy recommendations in six areas: human settlements, natural resource management, pollutants, environment and development, the social context underlying perceptions of environmental issues, and international organizational behavior. The *Action Plan* confirmed that environmental problems did not exist in isolation and that an integrative approach that looked at different sectors and actors and the links among them would be the only way to understand why environmental problems existed and how they could be solved.

Perhaps the most tangible and enduring legacy of the Stockholm conference was the creation of the United Nations Environment Programme (UNEP). The need for an international entity to act as a catalyst for environmental action within the UN system was clear, and UNEP was the response. Key tasks envisaged for UNEP included developing environmental information and assessment programs and exchanging and disseminating data on the seriousness of particular problems. UNEP was also to further international cooperation toward solutions for shared environmental problems, such as transboundary pollution issues. UNEP's headquarters were to be based in Nairobi, a marked departure from the previous institutional practice of siting UN agencies in the industrial countries. This decision, supported strongly by developing countries, was a way of encouraging the support of the South for Stockholm's environmental vision.

Stockholm will also be remembered as among the first global conferences where the stirrings of "civil society"—private, nongovernmental interests and groups—found resonance. For the first time, NGOs and other nongovernmental actors were prominently engaged in and around the conference. Their influence in environmental decision making would grow exponentially from this date.

*Perhaps the most tangible and enduring legacy of the Stockholm conference was the creation of the **United Nations Environment Programme (UNEP)***

In retrospect, the Stockholm conference helped make the environment a legitimate cause for both international and domestic attention and action. It aided the passage of national environmental legislation and the formation of environmental ministries and departments in many countries. It launched basic principles of international environmental law, a discipline without much previous history. It created UNEP, which proved to be unexpectedly influential in shaping the emergence of global environmental governance. Although Stockholm did not dwell extensively on global environmental concerns, much less force them onto an agenda requiring international action, it did provide a framework for international progress and thus paved the way for future efforts.

> Stockholm will also be remembered as among the first global conferences where the stirrings of *"civil society"*—private, nongovernmental interests and groups—found resonance.

Stockholm to Rio: Across New Frontiers

Although the Stockholm conference was an international event broadly concerned with the "human environment," the environmental concerns of the early 1970s were overwhelmingly local issues: local air and water pollution, highway and dam construction, strip-mining and clear-cutting, nuclear power plants, and so on. It would be a decade after Stockholm before chapter 2's agenda of global environmental challenges would take shape. Still, the years following Stockholm did see some important early actions addressing international environmental concerns.

Rising marine pollution and declining fish catches in many parts of the globe led to some of the earliest international actions. Because marine issues were so clearly ones requiring international responses, and because they were deemed to be politically ripe, much of the early international efforts for environmental cooperation focused on them. The Convention on the Prevention of Marine Pollution by Dumping of Wastes and Other Matter (London Dumping Convention, 1972) and the Convention on the Prevention of Pollution from Ships (MARPOL Convention, 1973) both addressed pollution of the oceans from ships.

Regional-scale air pollution, like marine pollution, was similarly being acknowledged as an international problem. Following concerns that emissions of sulfur and nitrogen oxides were spilling over national boundaries and causing acid rain, European countries decided to cooperate regarding the monitoring and exchange of information on such pollutants. The Convention on Long Range Transboundary Air Pollution (1979) was negotiated under the aegis of the UN Economic Commission for Europe.

In addition to tackling pollution issues, the 1970s saw early international activity aimed at nature and species protection. The Convention on the Protection of the World's Cultural and Natural Heritage (World Heritage Convention), signed in 1972, aimed to identify, protect, and preserve places of extraordinary natural or cultural significance. Some of the World Heritage Sites since designated include the Great Barrier Reef, Galapagos Natural Park, the Yellowstone National Park, the Taj Mahal, the Acropolis, and the Statue of Liberty.

The Convention on International Trade in Endangered Species of World Flora and Fauna (CITES) was another important international effort. The CITES convention, adopted in 1973, sought to police the growing trade in threatened wild species of plants and animals. Spurred to action by widespread attention to slaughter of African elephants for their ivory, countries turned to CITES as a way to restrict, and where necessary, ban, international trade in endangered species. Another concern requiring international cooperation was protection of migratory species, which led to the Convention on Conservation of Migratory Species of Wild Animals adopted in 1979. (A partial list of UN conferences and treaties is provided in the annex to chapter 4.)

In parallel with the development of these early treaties in the 1970s, the agenda of the major global concerns as we know it today was taking shape. Throughout the 1970s, a steady stream of publications with a planetary perspective emerged and called attention to global concerns. Most were authored by scientists with the goal of taking their findings and those of other colleagues to a larger audience.

There were also numerous reports from scientific groups, especially panels and committees organized by the International Council of Scientific Unions and its Scientific Committee on Problems of the Environment (SCOPE), the U.S. National Academy of Sciences, the International Union for the Conservation of Nature (IUCN), and UNEP. These reports included the now famous 1974 study by Rowland and Molina, explaining the potential of CFCs to deplete the ozone layer. (Their work remains the only environmental research to date to win a Nobel Prize.) Also among these documents was the pioneering Charney Report, which was published by the U.S. National Academy of Sciences in 1979 and which told us enough about the risks of climate change to raise alarms.[3] Such reports, including

Three Efforts in the 1970s to Call Attention to Global Challenges

"Over the past few years, the concept of the earth as a 'spaceship' has provided many people with an awareness of the finite resources and the complex natural relationships on which man depends for his survival. These realizations have been accompanied by concerns about the impacts that man's activities are having on the global environment. Some concerned individuals, including well-known scientists, have warned of both imminent and potential global environmental catastrophes."*

"Now that mankind is in the process of completing the colonization of the planet, learning to manage it intelligently is an urgent imperative. Man must accept responsibility for the stewardship of the earth. The word *stewardship* implies, of course, management for the sake of someone else. . . . [I]n practice [our] charge was clearly to define what should be done to maintain the earth as a place suitable for human life not only now, but also for future generations."**

"The deterioration of biological systems is not a peripheral issue of concern only to environmentalists. Our economic system depends on the earth's biological systems. Anything that threatens the viability of these biological systems threatens the global economy. Any deterioration in these systems represents a deterioration in the human prospect. . . . What is new today is the scale and speed at which biological resources are being impaired and destroyed. . . .

"The adjustments we must now make in consumption patterns, in population policy, and in the economic system if we are to preserve the biological underpinnings of the global economy are profound; they will challenge fully both human ingenuity and the human capacity for behavioral change."†

*Man's Impact on the Global Environment. 1970. The Report of the Study of Critical Environmental Problems. Cambridge, Mass: MIT Press, 4.

**Ward, B. and R. Dubos. 1972. *Only One Earth: The Care and Maintenance of a Small Planet*. New York: W. W. Norton, xiii.

†Brown, L. 1978. *The Twenty-Ninth Day: Accommodating Human Needs and Numbers to the Earth's Resources*. New York: W. W. Norton, 4.

the steady stream of publications from the Worldwatch Institute, collectively laid out the key issues.

Then, starting around 1980, a series of reports appeared seeking to pull together all of these issues into a coherent agenda for international action. These predominantly scientific efforts were designed to bring global challenges forcefully to the attention of governments. Collectively they stressed the major environmental concerns reviewed in chapter 2.

UNEP was active during this period both in nurturing this new and more ambitious agenda of global challenges and in building a foundation for the development of international environmental law as the principal

---

One Effort in 1980 to Frame the Global Environmental Agenda

The U.S. Council of Environmental Quality and Department of State presenting forecasts in 1980 of what could occur by 2000 absent societal responses: "Regional water shortages will become more severe. In the 1970–2000 period population growth alone will cause requirements for water to double in nearly half the world. . . . "Significant losses of world forests will continue over the next 20 years as demand for forest products and fuelwood increases. . . . The projections indicate that by 2000 some 40 percent of the remaining forest cover in [developing countries] will be gone.

"Serious deterioration of agricultural soils will occur worldwide, due to erosion, loss of organic matter, desertification, salinization, alkalinization, and waterlogging. Already, an area of cropland and grassland approximately the size of Maine is becoming barren wasteland each year, and the spread of desert-like conditions is likely to accelerate.

"Atmospheric concentrations of carbon dioxide and oxone-depleting chemicals are expected to increase at rates that could alter the world's climate and upper atmosphere significantly by 2050. Acid rain from increased combustion of fossil fuels (especially coal) threatens damage to lakes, solids, and crops. Radioactive and other hazardous materials present health and safety problems in increasing numbers of countries.

"Extinctions of plant and animal species will increase dramatically. Hundreds of thousands of species—perhaps as many as 20 percent of all species on earth—will be irretrievably lost as their habitats vanish, especially in tropical forests."*

*U.S. Council of Environmental Quality and Department of State. 1980. *The Global 2000 Report to the President*. Washington, D.C.: Government Printing Office, 2–3.

means to address them. In addition to taking the initiative on many of the reports just mentioned, it made estimates of deforestation and promoted strategies of action, convened the 1977 international conference on desertification, and supported the World Climate Program of the World Meteorological Organization, all in the 1970s.

UNEP also began developing a comprehensive series of environmental databases and information exchange procedures. These databases not only organized information for the international community—especially for developing countries that lacked their own scientific and technological capabilities and needed to rely on these sources as a foundation for national regulations—but also helped to mobilize and organize networks of scientists who were responsible for developing and administering the databases and who could advise and press governments on behalf of environmental protection.

The global environmental agenda thus emerged and moved forward due primarily to a relatively small, international leadership community in science, government, the United Nations, and NGOs. They took available opportunities to put these issues forward. By the mid-1980s a new and international agenda had been established in the sense that governments felt compelled to address collectively in some way to be credible. As a result, by the mid-1990s, a decade later, most of the major challenges discussed in chapter 2 had become the subjects of treaties, plans of action, or other international agreement. (These outcomes are summarized under Treaty Regimes and the Other Major Global Environmental Threats in chapter 4.)

Leaders in the scientific and NGO communities had excellent media access to keep the pressure on and keep the issues in the public eye. Action on

---

New Systems of Environmental Information Developed by UNEP

- GRID (Global Information Resource Database), which stores environmental data along local, national, regional, and global scales
- INFOTERRA, a global system of reference that networks 177 environmental information databases in separate nations and helps in information exchange and policy learning
- GEMS (Global Environmental Monitoring Systems), a satellite-based system to monitor oceanic and terrestrial trends
- IRPTC (International Registry of Potentially Toxic Chemicals), now developed as a clearinghouse on hazardous substances, chemical use, and safety

these issues in the 1980s was also spurred by a continuing series of high-visibility events that underscored the seriousness of environmental threats. The 1985 discovery of the "ozone hole" over Antarctica and ominous predictions of mounting skin cancers fanned public concerns. Scientific literature on global warming started entering everyday conversation; by the mid-1980s, the *New York Times* and other media outlets were editorializing on the threat. Mass disasters such as the 1984 methyl isocyanide gas leak at Union Carbide's Bhopal facility in India, the 1986 nuclear accident in the Chernobyl reactor, the 1989 *Exxon Valdez* oil spill, and the continuing high rates of deforestation in the tropics all made international headlines.

Building on established patterns, both domestic and international, the principal response of the international community to this global agenda was an escalation in the development of international environmental law. One of the first results was the Vienna Convention on the Protection of the Ozone Layer (1985), which was followed by its Montreal Protocol in 1987, aimed at preventing depletion of the ozone layer. Detailed steps for cooperation and time schedules on phasing out ozone-depleting substances were put in place, and their success showed that international urgency and commitment could work.

Another major treaty of the 1980s, the Basel Convention (1989) was aimed at the "control of trans-boundary movements of hazardous wastes and their disposal." The Convention established requirements of prior notice to countries to which wastes would be sent, written consent from them, and "environmentally sound management" as preconditions for legal trade.

UNEP was also using this period to lay the groundwork for what would become the World Commission on Environment and Development (WCED). In 1987, under the leadership of Norway's prime minister Gro Harlem Brundtland, WCED issued a seminal report titled *Our Common Future*. This report proved influential later on, especially at the 1992 Rio Earth Summit, due to its powerful advocacy of sustainable development.

> As we saw in chapter 1, the **Brundtland Commission** defined sustainable development as "development that meets the needs of present generations without compromising the ability of future generations to meet their needs."

As we saw in chapter 1, the Brundtland Commission defined sustainable development as "development that meets the needs of present generations without compromising the ability of future generations to meet their needs." It was not a new idea. The 1980 *World Conservation*

The Brundtland Commission: "Our Common Future"

The World Commission on Environment and Development (WCED) issued its seminal report, *Our Common Future,* in 1987. The commission was chaired by the Norwegian Prime Minister, Gro Harlem Brundtland, and is eponymously known as the Brundtland Commission. The report built upon the foundations of sustainable development from the *World Conservation Strategy* of 1980 and developed a new and lasting definition of the concept.

Sustainable development, the report said, is development that meets the needs of the present without compromising the ability of future generations to meet their own needs.

More important, however, was the powerful argument put forth that linked environmental degradation to poverty and the necessity of economic development in the developing world. The report, which was accepted and adopted by the United Nations General Assembly, called for a collective effort to address environmental threats and economic development goals as interrelated phenomena: "The 'environment' is where we live; and 'development' is what we all do in attempting to improve our lot in that abode. The two are inseparable. . . . Many of the development paths of the industrialized nations are clearly unsustainable. And the development decision of these countries, because of their great economic and political power, will have a profound effect on the ability of all peoples to sustain human progress for generations to come.

"Many critical survival issues are related to uneven development, poverty, and population growth. They all place unprecedented pressures on the planet's lands, waters, forests, and other natural resources, not least in the developing countries. The downward spiral of poverty and environmental degradation is a waste of opportunities and resources. . . . These links between poverty, inequality, and environmental degradation (require) a new era of economic growth that is . . . socially and environmentally sustainable."*

*World Commission on Environment and Development. 1987. *Our Common Future.* Oxford: Oxford University Press, xi–xii.

Strategy, authored by IUCN and UNEP, had been subtitled *Living Resource Conservation for Sustainable Development.* It contained chapters on sustainable development and the integration of environment with development. However, it was the Brundtland Commission's powerful use of the concept and acceptance of the report by the UN General Assembly that gave the term its new political salience.

Returning to the theme of the earlier Founex conference, the Brundtland Commission advocated the view that poverty alleviation and protecting the environment must go together. Poverty fuels ecological degradation by leaving the poor with little choice but to deplete resources for daily needs. Conversely, the poor are often the most vulnerable to environmental risks and ecological decline. Relieving poverty must be part of any overall environmental strategy, the WCED urged.

In 1989, to solve the puzzle of how actually to implement "sustainable development," the UN General Assembly announced it would sponsor a UN Conference on Environment and Development, which was to be held three years hence in Rio de Janeiro, Brazil. Its principal purpose was to "elaborate strategies and measures to halt and reverse the effects of environmental degradation in the context of increased national and international efforts to promote sustainable and environmentally sound development in all countries." Protection of the environment was thus to be filtered through the lens of sustainable development: environmental issues could not be separated from economic questions, and vice versa.

The conference organizers were charged with many tasks, from documenting world environmental trends and their trajectories over the two decades since the 1972 Stockholm conference to promoting new strategies to further development of international environmental law. The UN General Assembly asked the conference to examine the UN's own role as well and to elaborate new regional and global strategies of cooperation that might be pursued. The developing world was to receive particular attention in this endeavor.

This mandate, while somewhat similar to Stockholm's, was both more detailed and more comprehensive. The road to Rio was marked by extraordinary preparation and negotiations on a wide variety of global concerns: climate change, transboundary air pollution, deforestation, desertification, land degradation, biodiversity, environmentally sound management of biotechnology, forests, protection of oceans, seas and coastal areas, freshwater resources, hazardous wastes, toxic chemicals, poverty, and quality of life. The conference was to propose an Earth Charter, new institutional frameworks and legal tools, new financing mechanisms and economic incentives for environmental decisions, the reform of national accounting systems and pricing of goods, new sanctions and penalties for noncompliance, and new fora for information exchange, education, and environmental awareness. The task undertaken in the Rio conference's preparatory process was comprehensive.

The Earth Summit: A Peak on the Journey

The United Nations Conference on Environment and Development (UNCED) was held in Rio de Janeiro June 5 to June 18, 1992. The conference was attended by 178 nations, with 118 heads of state or government (there had been only two at Stockholm), 8,000 official delegates, nearly 1,400 NGOs represented by 3,000 accredited observers, 9,000 journalists, and approximately 15,000 to 20,000 visitors. The scale of the conference—soon dubbed the Earth Summit—was unprecedented.

Simultaneous events parallel to the official venues reflected an openness to incorporating NGOs and other representatives of civil society into global environmental policymaking. A Global Forum became a scene for leaders from civil society to meet, exchange ideas, and compare strategies. Another novel development was the initiation of an international Business Council for Sustainable Development, a pathbreaking effort to involve business and industry in the goals of sustainability. The head of the UNCED secretariat, Canadian Maurice Strong, reprising the leadership role he had in Stockholm, was himself a businessman, and he particularly emphasized the need to form strategic partnerships with business leaders.

In formal governmental spheres, the importance of UNCED was clear. The legitimacy and seriousness of the environment as a global issue were no longer in question. The political setting at Rio seemed ripe to translate the idea of sustainable development into practical policy solutions that many nations could implement both collectively and individually.

As at Stockholm, Rio dealt extensively with the relations between nations of the industrialized North and the underdeveloped South. Countries such as Malaysia asked tough questions of the industrialized nations, particularly the United States. How should the costs of environmental restoration and future protection in the developing world be shared? Who was more to be blamed for the rise in pollution and drawdown of natural resources: the rich nations because of their profligate consumption? or the poorer nations because of their population explosion? Which environmental issues deserved immediate priority: global environmental issues such as climate change and biodiversity? or livelihood issues such as access to freshwater, desertification, and food security? These debates informed the output of the UNCED deliberations.

In the end, the results of Rio were wide ranging and comprehensive. The answer to hard questions was, inevitably, "all of the above." A Rio Declaration elaborated 27 principles that should govern the future of environmental decision making, building on the Stockholm Declaration before it. These principles were the result of political compromises among nations of competing positions and interests, and one can see in most of them two viewpoints, often North and South, competing for dominance. The principles nonetheless represented collective international affirmations. Although they are guiding principles, which are not binding on nations, they can also be seen as reflections of emerging international environmental law.

> *The conference approved a path-breaking document called **Agenda 21,** which was a detailed blueprint for putting sustainable development into practice.*

In addition to the Rio Declaration, the conference approved a path-breaking document called *Agenda 21,* which was a detailed blueprint for putting sustainable development into practice. This nonbinding document, hailed as the most significant contribution of Rio, had 40 chapters and 115 program areas laid out over 800 pages and set forth a policy framework for all actors to implement sustainable development in everyday life. The document itself consisted of four broad areas:

- *Social and economic development* Highlighting international cooperation and assistance, poverty reduction, overconsumption, population trends, health, human settlements, and policymaking for sustainable development;

- *Conservation and management of resources for development* Addressing the issues of energy use, integrated land resource use, deforestation, desertification and drought, mountain ecosystems, agricultural needs and rural development, biodiversity, biotechnology, oceans, freshwaters, toxic chemicals, and hazardous and radioactive wastes;

- *Strengthening the role of major groups* Focusing on actors other than governments: women, youth, indigenous peoples, NGOs, business and industry, scientists, communities, workers, trade unions, and farmers;

- *Means of implementation* Addressing how international and national support should be organized, including a transfer to the South of financial resources and environment-friendly technology; building capacity through technical assistance, environmental education, and

Principles of the Rio Declaration

Principle 1. Human beings are at the center of concerns for sustainable development. They are entitled to a healthy and productive life in harmony with nature.

Principle 2. States have . . . the sovereign right to exploit their own resources pursuant to their own environmental and developmental policies, and the responsibility to ensure that activities within their jurisdiction or control do not cause damage to the environment of other States or of areas beyond the limits of national jurisdiction.

Principle 4. In order to achieve sustainable development, environmental protection shall constitute an integral part of the development process and cannot be considered in isolation from it.

Principle 7. States shall cooperate in a spirit of global partnership to conserve, protect and restore the health and integrity of the Earth's ecosystem. In view of the different contributions to global environmental degradation, States have common but differentiated responsibilities. The developed countries acknowledge the responsibility that they bear in the international pursuit of sustainable development in view of the pressures their societies place on the global environment and of the technologies and financial resources they command.

Principle 10. Environmental issues are best handled with the participation of all concerned citizens, at the relevant level. At the national level, each individual shall have appropriate access to information concerning the environment that is held by public authorities, including information on hazardous materials and activities in their communities, and the opportunity to participate in decision-making processes. States shall facilitate and encourage public awareness and participation by making information widely available. Effective access to judicial and administrative proceedings, including redress and remedy, shall be provided.

Principle 14. States should effectively cooperate to discourage or prevent the relocation and transfer to other States of any activities and substances that cause severe environmental degradation or are found to be harmful to human health.

Principle 15. In order to protect the environment, the precautionary approach shall be widely applied by States according to their capabilities. Where there are threats of serious or irreversible damage, lack of full scientific certainty shall not be used as a reason for postponing cost-effective measures to prevent environmental degradation.

Principle 16. National authorities should endeavor to promote the internalization of environmental costs and the use of economic instruments, taking into account the approach that the polluter should, in principle, bear the cost of pollution, with due regard to the public interest and without distorting international trade and investment.

Principle 17. Environmental impact assessment, as a national instrument, shall be undertaken for proposed activities that are likely to have a significant adverse impact on the environment and are subject to a decision of a competent national authority.

Principle 20. Women have a vital role in environmental management and development. Their full participation is therefore essential to achieve sustainable development.

Principle 22. Indigenous people and their communities and other local communities have a vital role in environmental management and development because of their knowledge and traditional practices. States should recognize and duly support their identity, culture and interests and enable their effective participation in the achievement of sustainable development.

Source: United Nations Environment Programme, www.unep.org.

scientific information; creating better environmental databases to bridge the data gaps between nations; and improving international environmental organizations, coordination, and legal processes.

Looking back on *Agenda 21*, two interesting trends appear. The first was the linking of poverty alleviation and official development assistance (ODA) with the broader goals of environmental protection. The Earth Summit called for a doubling of the industrial world's assistance to poorer countries to support implementation of *Agenda 21*. The second trend was the linking of the local and the global. Local actions in different parts of the world, facilitated by international organizations, governments, and businesses, were to be part of the collective response.

> The first was the linking of poverty alleviation and **official development assistance (ODA)** with the broader goals of environmental protection.

Although *Agenda 21* was impressive, its scope and comprehensiveness resulted in a very ambitious agenda for governments that made the whole enterprise heavily dependent on strong leadership from major countries, adequate financing, and effective institutional arrangements for follow-up. Unfortunately, as we shall see, none of these materialized in the years after Rio.

To help implement *Agenda 21*, a new institution, the Commission on Sustainable Development (CSD), was created by the United Nations shortly after Rio. Part of the UN's Economic and Social Council (ECOSOC), the CSD was charged with the task of "monitoring the implementation of *Agenda 21*." Headquartered in New York, this institution was to consider information given by governments, act as a forum for exchange, and enable coordination among the various groups mentioned in *Agenda 21*. However, like ECOSOC itself, the CSD has proven to be long on dialogue and speech making but short on stimulating action.

In addition to *Agenda 21* and the Rio Declaration, several important treaties were initiated at Rio. In the UN Framework Convention on Climate Change (UNFCCC), nations agreed that protecting climate was a "common concern of mankind" and established a goal of preventing dangerous anthropogenic interference with the global climate system. Industrial countries were exhorted to return their climate-altering emissions to 1990 levels and to have plans of action to this end.

The Convention on Biological Diversity (CBD) was another framework treaty focused on protecting biodiversity. Nations agreed on the need for conservation of biodiversity, sustainable use of resources, access to genetic resources, fair and equitable benefit sharing, and transfer of technologies. Southern nations were able to express their concerns about patenting of life forms found in their borders, such as the use of tropical plants as the basis for pharmaceuticals in the industrialized counties, and northern countries were able to note their concerns for the conservation and sustainable use of endangered and threatened species.

Nonbinding *Forest Principles* and commitments to develop international conventions on desertification, fishing in the high seas, and land-based sources of marine pollution were also agreed to at Rio.

Major financial support was needed for developing countries to comply with new treaties. The Global Environment Facility (GEF) was set up before Rio in 1990 with a goal to provide financing for global environmental objectives, and the Earth Summit gave it strong support. Though broader today, the original principle for GEF funding was that financial assistance was to be given to meet the

The Global Environment Facility (GEF) was set up before Rio in 1990 with a goal to provide financing for global environmental objectives, and the Earth Summit gave it strong support.

"global incremental costs" of specific projects—those costs required to realize global environmental benefits that are over and above what a country would spend to reap purely national benefits. GEF funding was therefore not meant to substitute for normal development aid or for the host country's own financing but to supplement it by paying the costs of going beyond traditional development to realize global environmental benefits.

These results at the Earth Summit seemed tangible evidence of international commitment. Yet critics cite what could have happened but did not. No Earth Charter was agreed to. There was no forestry convention, only the nonbinding set of principles that were wholly inadequate to deal with growing threats to forests. The treaties on climate and biodiversity were only frameworks, requiring subsequent efforts if they were to have teeth to them. The commitment to support *Agenda 21* with major new funding remained to be implemented (and in the end was not). And the Earth Summit gave scant attention to measures needed to ensure follow-up action post-Rio.

Yet the Earth Summit, even with its failures and controversies, did offer some promise of a new era of global cooperation. Nonstate actors, from NGO groups to businesses, were involved in creating strategies and discussing avenues of common endeavor. Sustainable development was now articulated and given political legitimacy as a defining concept for national and global progress. Principles of partnership and assistance between rich and poor were agreed. Maurice Strong, the extraordinary secretary-general of the summit, reminded delegates that the Earth Summit was not an end in itself but a new beginning. Whether the Earth Summit would indeed usher in a new era of global environmental governance was a question that the next decade would soon answer. Unfortunately, most observers today would agree that Rio's deficiencies were not corrected in the decade that followed, and the potential offered by the Earth Summit was not realized.

Rio to Johannesburg: A Zigzag Trail

The decade after the Earth Summit saw the momentum of treaty development continue unabated. Building on the commitment at Rio, the UN Convention to Combat Desertification (1994) provided an innovative framework for national planning aimed at desertification and drought, particularly in Africa. The Rotterdam Convention (1998) on Prior Informed Consent established a procedure by which trade in hazardous chemicals and pesticides could be regulated by ensuring that receiving countries approved the imports in advance. The Stockholm Convention on Persistent Organic Pollutants (2001) provided a mechanism for prohibiting or regulating the release of POPs that have the potential to cause severe health threats such as cancers, immune deficiencies, and hormonal disruption. The Cartagena Protocol on Biosafety (2000) under the convention on biodiversity, aimed to regulate trade in living genetically modified organisms (GMOs), also uses the prior informed consent approach. It requires risk assessment studies and prior information procedures before nations import such products.

Perhaps the most well known of the treaties negotiated in the years following the Earth Summit was the Kyoto Protocol (1997) to the UN Framework Convention on Climate Change. The Kyoto Protocol called for individual commitments by industrial nations to reduce emissions of six greenhouse gases by 2008–2012, which were expected to lead to an overall reduction of greenhouse gas emissions to levels 5 percent below 1990 levels by 2008–2012, the so-called first commitment period.

Despite this progress on the environmental law front, the decade after Rio also saw a changing tide in global affairs. In 1994, negotiations concluded in the Uruguay Round of the General Agreement on Tarrifs and Trade (GATT), and in 1995 a new international organization, the World Trade Organization (WTO), came into being. The purpose of the WTO is to facilitate increased trade in goods and services between nations by reducing trade barriers and distortions. This increase in international trade is a leading aspect of the broader economic globalization now under way.

Another aspect of globalization is the huge growth in the flow of private investment, especially from industrial countries to developing countries. Such investments have increased severalfold and exceeded $200 billion in 2000. Meanwhile, ODA from rich nations to poor declined after Rio, rather

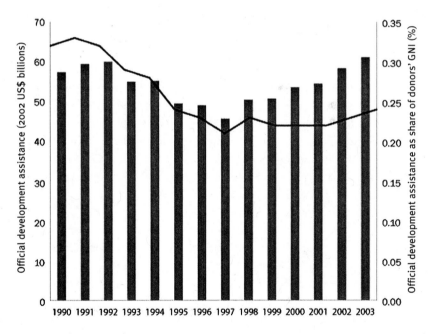

Figure 3.1 Official development assistance is now rising again, but still too little. Source: OECD Development Assistance Committee.

than the promised increase. It was 2003 before ODA recovered to its 1992 level. The United States and other industrial countries concentrated their efforts in this period on trade promotion and economic challenges, while in foreign policy regional conflicts, peacekeeping missions, and international terrorism all drew attention away from the policies and agreements forged at Rio.

In sum, the decade after Rio saw a breakdown in the international leadership called for at the Rio Earth Summit. Progress was at best slow, and efforts overall fell short of expectations. It took 13 years to move from the signing of the Climate Convention at Rio to the entry into force in 2005 of the Kyoto Protocol (and the United States, the largest emitter of greenhouse gases, has refused to ratify the Protocol). Even less progress has been made under the biodiversity and desertification conventions and in forging effective agreements to protect marine fisheries and world forests. Many observers believe that much of the ground gained at Rio was lost.

The Johannesburg Summit: Too Steep an Incline

In December 2000, eight years after the Rio Earth Summit, the United Nations called for a new summit, to take place in Johannesburg in 2002, to review the commitments of Rio and hopefully to rekindle fresh political and financial commitments for sustainable development and *Agenda 21*.

In the run-up to what became the World Summit for Sustainable Development (WSSD) in September 2002, almost everyone accepted the proposition that the Rio agreements had not been effectively implemented and that this failure was due in part to the industrial countries not fulfilling the expectation created at Rio, including the expectation that ODA would be greatly increased to help implement *Agenda 21*. For many, therefore, WSSD was to be about implementation.

From the outset, however, Johannesburg lacked the leadership and skillful preparation seen at Rio. In the end, the outcomes of WSSD bore little resemblance to the specific, monitorable plans of action hoped for by many. The United States and several other governments successfully resisted proposals for strict targets and timetables. Instead, broad, general agreements were reached to endorse the 2000 UN Millennium Development Goal aimed at cutting in half the proportion of the world's people lacking access to basic sanitation by 2015, to minimize the adverse affects of toxic chemicals by 2020, to restore fish stocks "where possible, not later than 2015," and to achieve by 2010 a significant reduction in the current rate of loss of biodiversity.

The major discussions at Johannesburg were less about concrete environmental goals and commitments and more about bringing together the three dimensions of sustainable development—the "triple bottom line" of economy, environment, and society. Here also the results were not viewed as impressive. The social and economic dimensions of sustainable development tended to dominate, and Johannesburg accurately reflected a world badly divided on key issues: corporate accountability, globalization and the WTO, trade and trade subsi-

*Instead, broad, general agreements were reached to endorse the **2000 UN Millennium Development Goal** aimed at cutting in half the proportion of the world's people lacking access to basic sanitation by 2015, to minimize the adverse affects of toxic chemicals by 2020, to restore fish stocks "where possible, not later than 2015," and to achieve by 2010 a significant reduction in the current rate of loss of biodiversity.*

Millennium Development Goals

The Millennium Development Goals (MDGs) were adopted in 2000 by the Millennium Assembly of the United Nations. They brought together a series of quantitative, time-bound targets developed out of the several global conferences sponsored by the United Nations in the 1990s and the work of the OECD's Development Assistance Committee. Key among the goals are commitments to:

- Halve by 2015 the proportion of people whose income is less than $1 per day
- Halve by 2015 the proportion of people who suffer from hunger
- Ensure by 2015 universal primary education
- Eliminate gender disparity in education by 2015
- Halve by 2015 the proportion of people without sustainable access to safe drinking water and sanitation
- Integrate the principles of sustainable development into country policies and programs and reverse the loss of environmental resources.

The MDGs have generated more attention and support than previous efforts in these areas. They also demonstrate the difficulty of framing quantitative, time-bound targets in the environmental area.

U.N. Development Programme. 2003. *Human Development Report 2003*. Oxford: Oxford University Press.

dies, energy and climate, development priorities and aid, and many others. In the end delegates could agree mostly on platitudes and on-the-one-hand, on-the-other-hand.

In sum, the WSSD failed to embrace new verifiable goals or to advance significantly efforts for the protection of the global environment. On a more positive side, it did initiate, haltingly, a new approach to global governance based on the notion of "partnerships" between different actors. Governments at WSSD presented specific national plans for sustainable development projects, referred to as "Type II initiatives," that would involve participation by some combination of national actors, international business, and NGOs. Such intentions were fraught with political undercurrents. Some observers saw Type II initiatives as a means of avoiding Type I initiatives such as the time-bound governmental commitments they had hoped Johannesburg would generate. Governments refused to define clearly who could be their counterparts for development projects, leaving the door open for state-created NGOs. Also, a disappointingly small number of new specific partnerships were actually unveiled at the conference.

The international NGO community turned out in force for Johannesburg, reflecting its growing vitality. The business community was deeply involved, often quite positively, building on the start at Rio. The developing countries (and development assistance organizations) and the business community left Johannesburg far more pleased than the environmental community, which saw little of positive note at Johannesburg.

Concluding Observations

The story of developments from Stockholm to Johannesburg is one that cries out for explanation. The story begins with the excitement of a new beginning at Stockholm in 1972, moves strongly forward with hope and expectation through the defining of an agenda of global challenges a decade later, and on to the Rio Earth Summit in 1992 where what needs to be done to meet those challenges is rigorously and comprehensively defined. But then, after Rio, momentum begins to flag, progress becomes slow and halting, promise fades and hopes go unrealized—yet the problems sketched in chapter 2 persist, growing in both scale and urgency.

Agenda-setting and the mobilization of concern were effectively promoted in the 1970s and 1980s by transnational networks of NGOs and scientists, who took advantage of well-publicized environmental disasters to sketch how environmental threats were interconnected and to suggest policy responses to address them. But a variety of problems emerged in the 1990s when governments tried to mobilize political and economic resources to live up to their international commitments. We need to understand how this happened if we are going to correct it. As with other complex historical processes, these developments do not have a simple or single explanation, and events are too close at hand to offer assured answers. But some things do seem reasonably clear, at least in retrospect. The first is that many of the global environmental threats reviewed in chapter 2 are inherently difficult for both politicians and the public. For those of us in the affluent world, these threats tend to be remote from our daily lives, both temporarily and geographically. They are unfolding gradually (recall the proverbial frog in the slowly warming pot), and they tend to be technically complex and difficult to understand. By contrast, the domestic issues that drove the original Earth Day in 1970 involved obnoxious and visible environmental insults—in your face and in your neighborhood. The protection of the ozone layer is one global issue that was different—the threat of skin cancer was current and highly motivational to sunbathers, for example. The ozone depletion threat was thus more like the immediate environmental issues of the early 1970s. (The status of the global warming issue is now slowly changing as the public is becoming aware of the serious changes already under way.)

Because the global challenges tend to have weak domestic constituencies, politicians tend not to give them priority when it comes to funds, nor are they willing to take on powerful corporate interests (for example, in the energy, transportation, and chemical industries) often vested in the status quo. Meanwhile, the treaty-making process is allowed to plunge ahead because both governments and businesses understand the many weaknesses of international environmental law and know that they can almost always ensure toothless treaties if they like.

These inertial forces were given full reign in the period after the Rio Earth Summit due to a confluence of unfortunate circumstances. Martin Khor, director of the Third World Network and a leading critic of current globalization processes, has asked why the implementation of *Agenda 21* and other agreements reached at the Rio Earth Summit has "largely failed." "The reason for failure is not to be found in the sustainable development paradigm [forged at Rio]; rather, the paradigm was not given the chance to be implemented. Instead, intense competition came from a rival—the countervailing paradigm of globalization, driven by the industrialized North and its corporations, that has swept the world in recent years. This is perhaps the most basic factor causing the failure to realize the [Rio] objectives."[4] The ascendancy of the market-based globalization paradigm and the marginalization of the sustainable development paradigm have both resulted from "the strong support and aggressive advocacy of the powerful countries," Khor believes.

In the years since Rio, the governments of the large-economy, G8 countries have indeed vigorously pursued the market globalization agenda while badly neglecting the Earth Summit agenda and its program to realize sustainable development. Market-based globalization has been seen by many of its advocates as eliminating the need to take the Rio agenda seriously. "Trade not aid" has become a Washington mantra.

This said, the eclipse of the Rio Earth Summit commitments has surely been brought about by more than the ascendancy of the globalization paradigm. Many hoped that the post–Cold War period would bring a peace dividend of financial and political resources that could be applied to promoting environmental and development objectives. Instead, the United States and others have been enmeshed in a series of military and peacekeeping engagements, now embracing the fight against terrorism and the war in Iraq, that have consumed much of the available time, energy, and money. The peacekeeping budget of the United Nations began escalating rapidly after the end of the Cold War.

A related factor has been that the Rio agenda has struggled to move forward during a period in which the United States has shifted strongly in a conservative direction. The consensus in Washington has been increasingly negative on multilateralism, environmental regulation, the United Nations, foreign aid, and treaties and similar agreements, and, indeed, government itself. Grover Norquist, the leader of the powerful Washington activists on the political right, noted in 2005 that "what holds together the conservative movement" is that "they all want the government to go away."[5]

The view from Europe is not so bleak, and were we writing from a European perspective at this juncture we would be more inclined to emphasize the impressive steps being taken in the European Union to address the global warming threat, regulate toxic chemicals, and expand assistance to the developing world. From that perspective we would perhaps see the process from Stockholm to Johannesburg in a brighter light. For example, the efforts of the last 30 years have contributed to a large-scale shift in international politics by extending participation in environmental diplomacy to national environmental agencies, NGOs, and networks of scientists. These efforts have promoted broader processes of social learning and the construction of new, more comprehensive conceptual frameworks for global environmental governance. Issues have been clarified and popularized, and new approaches to environmental policymaking have been introduced. New norms of environmental protection have been diffused, and participating states have been encouraged to endorse them and to apply them nationally. International environmental problems are now firmly embedded on the international agenda, in fact far more strongly than many anticipated in 1972. Moreover, the perspective with which environmental problems are widely viewed has expanded from one where problems are addressed discretely to a new perspective that sees interconnected problems requiring a wide array of governance measures for their management.

These changes are significant and provide a basis for more effective action in the future.

IV

Environmental Accord: Treaties and International Environmental Law

THE JOURNEY FROM STOCKHOLM TO JOHANNESBURG TELLS US HOW WE GOT where we are today. In the next two chapters we look in more detail at the landscape that this three-decade journey has produced—the treaty regimes, the actors and institutions, and the way that all of these come together in the policymaking process and in voluntary, "bottom-up" initiatives by nongovernmental organizations (NGOs), businesses, and others. We focus first in this chapter on the treaties and the international environmental law of which treaties are a part. It is a good place to begin, for as we saw in chapter 3 as we journeyed from Stockholm to Johannesburg, the international community's first attempt at global environmental governance has been predominantly an effort to develop international environmental law.

International Law and Collective Action: The Basics

As we saw earlier, international environmental law embodies two classes of law, hard law and soft law. Hard law consists largely of treaties—legally binding agreements among nations—that are ratified by governments. Treaties are typically implemented nationally with legislation that provides for their administration and enforcement. In chapter 3 we touched upon many treaties that have been adopted in recent years to address global environmental challenges.

Soft law consists of nonbinding guidelines adopted in international processes, such as the Rio Declaration and the Forest Principles adopted at the Earth Summit or the chemical testing protocols developed by the Organization for Economic Cooperation and Development (OECD). They typically lack formal means of enforcement and are more like norms or exhortations than laws.

Environmental treaties are often referred to as multilateral environmental agreements (MEAs). Treaties can take the form of broad conventions or more specific and typically action-orientated protocols. Or they can codify and advance international law in a broad area, like the Law of the Sea. Major amendments to treaties typically require ratification by governments. A treaty or a set of related treaties and attendant arrangements are sometimes referred to as a regime, such as the climate regime, but the regime concept is also used more broadly.

Another distinction that is important in international law is the difference between signing and ratifying a treaty. When a government signs a treaty it merely indicates preliminary support for the commitments written in the treaty. For example, in the U.S. system, the executive branch acting alone can sign treaties. Ratification is the process by which the domestic legislature or rule-making body approves the treaty and converts it into domestic law. In the United States ratification is done by the Senate, where a two-thirds majority vote is required. These processes underscore that adoption of treaty commitments is voluntary and thus does not entail any sacrifice of national sovereignty, a point reinforced by the fact that nations can leave a treaty at any time.

Regimes, Broadly Defined

While most global environmental governance takes place through formal treaties and related institutions, these are not the only way to measure the level of coordination and cooperation taking place between states in the international system. A key concept in the area of international cooperation is that of "regimes." Regimes include a variety of formal and informal phenomena that shape or limit the behavior of nations. Stephen D. Krasner defines international regimes as "principles, norms, rules, and decision-making procedures."

Principles—beliefs of fact, causation and rectitude
Norms—standards of conduct and obligations
Rules—specifically enacted agreements
Decision-making procedures—the practices and routines of discussing and implementing policy.

continued

continued

Regimes are an interesting and important limitation to the concept of anarchy in the international system. While there may be no overarching global authority or government, the anarchical nature of the system is often mitigated by nations following and abiding by regularized and widely accepted series of regimes that allow for some level of continuity and stability in their relations. Regimes can also be thought of as social institutions created among nations.

The analysis of regimes, known generally as regime theory, has primarily dealt with the creation of regimes and cooperation among nations at the international level. While the concept of regimes is thus broad, like global governance, the word is also commonly used to refer more narrowly to the work associated with specific international agreements.

Krasner, S. 1985. Structural causes and regime consequences: Regimes as intervening variables. In *International Regimes,* ed. Stephen D. Krasner. Ithaca, N.Y.: Cornell University Press.

Treaties "enter into force"—that is, their terms become legally binding—after the ratification by a stipulated number of countries, which varies by treaty. For instance, the 1978 MAR-POL Convention governing operational oil pollution treaties required ratification by 15 states with a combined merchant fleet of not less than 50% of shipping by gross tonnage, and the Kyoto Protocol required ratification by 55 Annex I states (industrialized countries and Russia) accounting for at least 55% of the total 1990 carbon dioxide emissions from Annex I states.

*A treaty or a set of related treaties and attendant arrangements are sometimes referred to as a **regime**, such as the climate regime, but the regime concept is also used more broadly.*

Since, as we noted in chapter 3, the principal activity in the field of global environmental governance has been the development of international law, it follows that the governments of nation-states have been and remain far and away the principal actors. The principle of sovereignty guarantees that all nations are equal in the limited sense that no nation can be bound by a treaty without its consent.

As the leading casebook on international environmental law has noted: "Within the more sophisticated nation-States, there is a well-developed system for creating and enforcing law. In the most robust national systems, the legislative and executive powers are accountable under constitutions enforced by a judiciary with the power to issue authoritative and binding interpretations of existing law. National legislatures can create law of general applicability, which binds even those who may disagree with it. Increasingly throughout the world, citizens have the right to participate in national lawmaking—through referenda, legislative lobbying, and the election of representatives. Nation-States also have the power to implement and enforce the laws they create, and specific mechanisms often exist for citizens to participate here as well. The international law-making system is far less developed. Under the principles of international law established by Hugo Grotius and his successors, each nation-State is independent and sovereign. No supra-national legislature exists with the power to create law applicable to the entire world. Moreover, States are the primary subjects of international law. Few international regimes allow the active participation of non-State actors in lawmaking. As a general rule, no State may be bound by any international obligation without its consent, although consent may sometimes be inferred."[1]

Of course, in essentially every other context nations are decidedly unequal, and powerful nations determined to use international law to achieve a particular goal can and often do find incentives and disincentives sufficient to bring about participation and compliance by otherwise reluctant nations. Yet blatantly violating international obligations undermines a country's legitimacy, and makes it more difficult to get other countries to voluntarily acquiesce to its wishes on other matters in the future.

Although nations are the principal legal actors in making international environmental policy, they respond to pressure from a number of additional actors, including other nations, the United Nations and other international organizations, scientists, NGOs, and, notably, their own business sectors. The years of multilateral environmental governance have contributed to the legitimation and inclusion of such new nonstate actors. International environmental politics can be thought of as a "two-level game" where one playing field is the international arena and the other is national (domestic) politics. Many groups such as business organizations and NGOs vie for influence at both levels.

Different nations have a variety of justifiably different concerns and national interests. Consequently, achieving effective rules requires compromise

Theory of Collective Action

"Rational, self-interested individuals will not act to achieve their common or group interests."*

Mancur Olson argued that many of the prevailing arguments, in what is now generally known as Rational Choice Theory were flawed in their conclusions that actors would necessarily choose to cooperate on issues of common or public interest.

Olson demonstrated that actors' willingness to engage in collective action is strongly dependent upon the relative costs and benefits of action or inaction to specific actors. For example, while reduction of sulfur emissions would likely reduce acid rain, which would benefit all by reducing water pollution, ground pollution, and infrastructure decay, the costs of such collective action are not necessarily borne equally by all actors. Actors with a large stake in sulfur-emitting industries may have to pay high and concentrated costs to reduce emissions, negatively affecting their profitability. The actors that will gain from reduced sulfur emissions and acid rain, the public, will see diffuse benefits (measured both in temporal and monetary terms). The argument underpinning the strength of special interests is that small and dedicated lobbies, who have much at stake, tend to win out over the larger public good.

Olsen also noted that there was tremendous temptation by actors to avoid the costs of cooperation while still reaping the benefits. This is called the free rider problem. Actors may calculate that collective action will be taken by others to address a common interest problem without the need for their own sacrifice or contribution. The free rider may then enjoy the benefits of collective action while evading their own share of the costs. For example, a regional group of 10 advanced states all suffer from the effects of acid rain. The 10 states negotiate a treaty to reduce sulfur emissions that contribute to acid rain. Nine states ratify the treaty while the tenth state declines. The efforts of the nine states to reduce sulfur emissions are successful and acid rain is reduced for the entire region. The nine ratifying states all paid the costs of sulfur emission reductions. The tenth state was able to enjoy the benefits of reduced acid rain while shouldering none of the costs—riding free. This result can harm continued and future collective action since other states will, rightfully so, feel they are disproportionately bearing costs of action being avoided by others.

*Olson, M. 1965. *The Logic of Collective Action: Public Goods and the Theory of Groups*. Cambridge: Harvard University Press.

between the aspirations of different countries. In chapter 3 we reviewed many of the North–South tensions and disagreements that recur in international negotiations. For example, industrial countries tend to focus on efforts to manage the problems in isolation by developing international regimes to address them. Developing countries are more concerned with mitigating the social pressures that can generate environmental harm and placing issues in a developmental context. As the British rock star Sting noted, "If I were a Brazilian without land or money or the means to feed my children, I would be burning the rainforest too."

Not discussed in chapter 3 were the so-called countries in transition, which became independent after the collapse of the Soviet bloc and have only begun to assert themselves in international negotiations. Formerly centrally planned economies, they tend to express concern with a wide array of environmental problems, many stemming from their legacy of extensive chemical pollution as well as regional transboundary problems.

Multilateral environmental diplomacy has a long history. The first treaties dealing with environmental topics were adopted in Europe in the 1870s. The following figure depicts the dramatic growth in numbers of environmental treaties.

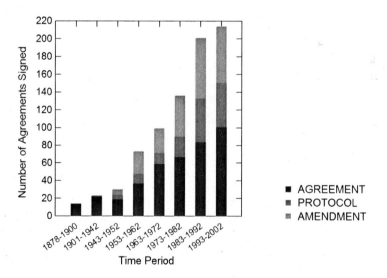

Figure 4.1 Data derived from Ronald B. Mitchell, 2003. *International Environmental Agreements Website,* http://www.uoregon.edu/~iea and described in Ronald B. Mitchell, 2003. International environmental agreements: A survey of their features, formation, and effects. *Annual Review of Environment and Resources.*

A growing range of activities have become subject to environmental treaties. Until the 1960s the majority of treaties addressed problems of over-fishing and species conservation. With the onset of global environmental crises in the late 1960s, attention turned to various aspects of pollution. Recent decades have seen environmental treaties take on increasingly bigger problems, such as climate change and biodiversity loss. The following figure documents the evolving focus of environmental treaties over time.

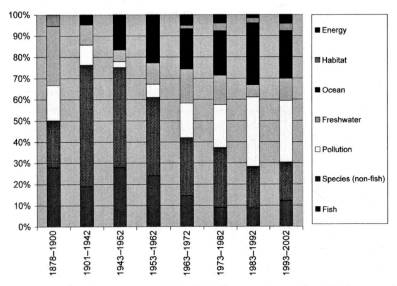

Figure 4.2 Data derived from Ronald B. Mitchell, 2003. *International Environmental Agreements Website,* http://www.uoregon.edu/~iea and described in Ronald B. Mitchell, 2003. International environmental agreements: A survey of their features, formation, and effects. *Annual Review of Environment and Resources.*

The Ozone Layer Protection Regime: The Little Engine That Could

The efforts associated with the 1985 Vienna Convention for the Protection of the Ozone Layer and its 1987 Montreal Protocol show how the treaty system just described should work. Indeed, they show global environmental governance at its best. Virtually all observers agree that the shining example of success in our area has been the effort to protect and restore Earth's ozone layer. It is important to understand how and why this success occurred, and much can be learned by tracing how the international community has addressed one of the major global challenges.

The ozone protection case highlights the roles of different actors and political forces in shaping multilateral environmental governance. It highlights the interplay of domestic and international forces. Whereas domestic actions successfully reduced threats to stratospheric ozone in the 1970s, these domestic efforts actually complicated the international coordination at subsequent stages because different countries were locked into different types of regulation. The ozone example also brings out the interplay of science, institutions, and the goals of the private sector.

We will follow the ozone-layer protection process through its various stages. Numerous analysts have outlined the stages in the life of an international environmental regime. We break the convention, or protocol, process down into four stages: (1) problem identification, fact finding, and agenda setting; (2) negotiation, bargaining, and agreement on what actions to take; (3) formal adoption; and (4) implementation, monitoring, assessment, and strengthening.

Problem Identification, Fact Finding, and Agenda Setting

This first stage takes us from the point at which a threat is spotted to the point where there is a tacit agreement among governments to do something to counter it. Scientists very often bring the issue forward to the attention of the public and policymakers. Sometimes "focusing events" dramatize that the problem is real, not just scientific speculation. Environmental groups, scientists, and government staff members typically work together to make the threat a public issue.

> We break the **convention**, or **protocol, process** down into four stages: (1) problem identification, fact finding, and agenda setting; (2) negotiation, bargaining, and agreement on what actions to take; (3) formal adoption; and (4) implementation, monitoring, assessment, and strengthening.

Through their policy entrepreneurship and advocacy, they move the threat onto the agenda that governments feel obligated to address. The first thing governments typically do is to commission more research and fact-finding.

In the case of ozone depletion, the threat was spotted in 1974 when Molina and Rowland published their research showing that chlorofluorocarbons (CFCs), though highly stable compounds in the troposphere, could release chlorine in the hostile environment of the stratosphere. The chlorine would in turn set off a chain reaction that would deplete the ozone there. CFCs and similar chemicals were in widespread use at the time as aerosol propellants (spray cans), refrigerants, and solvents, so the Molina-Rowland hypothesis led to intensive research efforts by scientists in and out of government. The media, environmental groups, and others raised the issue's visibility. Then, in 1977, the United States, Canada, and the Nordic countries called upon the United Nations Environment Programme (UNEP) to undertake a major fact-finding and issue-definition exercise. So between 1974 and 1977 the ozone depletion issue moved from being only a question of science onto the intergovernmental agenda.

Several developments in this first stage of the ozone regime process reflect patterns now common in global environmental governance. One pattern is the importance of good science and careful environmental monitoring in bringing issues forward and laying the groundwork for effective action. The role of science and scientists in the policy process is an immensely complex issue. The scientific content of public policy issues is increasing generally, and nowhere is this more prominent than in the area of the global environment. There is little hope of successfully addressing the difficult challenges reviewed in chapter 2 without rigorous scientific research and monitoring and without leadership from scientists themselves. Scientists often complain that they are not listened to, which can be true, yet it is also true that many scientists are reluctant to become engaged (embroiled, they would say) in the public policy process. They are not trained for it, and it is not what they *do:* they do science, not policy. This reluctance is linked to a persistent, inescapable reality of the science–policy interface: rarely will an issue be free of scientific disagreement, and rarely will it be free of scientific uncertainty. Scientific disagreements and uncertainties (unknowns) are very positive features of the scientific enterprise, but in the policy process they lead to difficult and often very contentious debates and arguments. Which scientific claim is the most reliable? Granted that there will always be uncertainties, how much knowledge is required to justify policy action?

These difficulties can be surmounted to some degree by having "decision rules," such as the Precau-

*Difficulties can be surmounted to some degree by having "decision rules," such as the **Precautionary Principle**, and by having formal processes in which leading scientists themselves sift through the data, process analyses and perspectives, and make their judgments known to policymakers as a group.*

The Precautionary Principle

One of the fundamental problems in global environmental governance is the level of uncertainty that exists in the science, economics, and policy prescriptions of environmental threats and solutions. Because of scientific uncertainty, the Precautionary Principle emerged. The principle has been adopted in several major environmental conventions of the United Nations and the European Union. Set out in the Framework Convention on Climate Change, the Rio Declaration, and the UN Global Compact, the principle states that "where there are threats of serious or irreversible damage, lack of full scientific certainty shall not be used as a reason for postponing cost-effective measures to prevent environmental harm." It includes several key concepts:

Preventative anticipation Taking action if necessary before full scientific proof is available

Proportionality of response Selecting degrees of restraint that are not unduly costly

Burden of proof Placing the onus of proof of safety on those creating the threat or risk

tionary Principle, and by having formal processes in which leading scientists themselves sift through the data, process analyses and perspectives, and make their judgments known to policymakers as a group. This is a major feature of the work of science academies around the world, such as the U.S. National Academy of Sciences. In other cases ad hoc institutions are created, such as the Intergovernmental Panel on Climate Change, a group of scientists and other analysts created by governments to provide the best information and research available on the climate issue to policymakers and the public.

A second common pattern reflected in the early development of the ozone issue is the coalescing, first, of scientists and then other experts into what has been called an "epistemic community"—experts who

A second common pattern reflected in the early development of the ozone issue is the coalescing, first, of scientists and then other experts into what has been called an "epistemic community"— experts who share common values and information and who are working together loosely to improve scientific and public understanding on an issue.

share common values and information and who are working together loosely to improve scientific and public understanding on an issue. As was true in the ozone case, the development of an epistemic community is often followed closely by the formation of an "advocacy coalition," a loose confederation of scientists, NGOs, bureaucrats, journalists, and opinion leaders seeking to move the issue onto the public agenda.

It is difficult to overstate the importance of environmental and other NGOs as actors in the policy process, particularly at the earlier stages. Whether they are policy research centers and "think tanks" or traditional environmental advocacy groups or direct action campaigners sponsoring boycotts and similar efforts, these groups have proven essential in bridging the gap between scientists and policymakers and in working with the media to bring issues to wide public attention.

A further point to note about the early development of the ozone issue is that it only became a serious matter for international action when it was taken up by nation-states. The formation of a "lead states coalition," in this case represented by the United States, Canada, and the Nordic countries, means that the issue has been taken up by governments, and in a world of sovereign nations, that is essential.

A final observation regarding the birth of the ozone regime is that, as in other cases, the nations promoting the agreement took their case to the UN system for action, in this case to UNEP. Indeed, essentially the entire corpus of international environmental law is a creation of the United Nations—born, nurtured, and maintained through processes carried out under UN auspices. For a small, underfunded, and often marginalized UN agency, UNEP was remarkably successful in its role as midwife to an outpouring of international environmental treaties.

Negotiation, Bargaining, and Agreement on Actions to Be Taken

The second stage in the treaty process, in the now standard convention-protocol model, typically involves international negotiations (under UN auspices) leading first to a "framework convention," which usually provides only general findings and policies, statements of broad goals, and institutional and governance arrangements. The more difficult negotiations are reserved for the more specific and action-oriented protocols that follow. (Not all efforts at regime formation survive this second stage, as the early and fruitless attempts to forge a global forests convention make clear.)

After declining in the 1970s, CFC use began climbing again in the 1980s, sparking new international concern and demands for additional action. Consumer decisions were proving incapable of addressing all the uses of CFCs, and nations were unwilling to unilaterally jeopardize their national industries by tighter domestic regulation. The process of controlling CFC use thus turned inevitably to building a multilateral regulatory system where issues of equity among countries and timetables for phasing CFC use down and then out could be negotiated and resolved by all the countries with a stake in the outcome.

UNEP, showing leadership here as it would later, launched the second stage of the process by calling for international negotiations in 1981. In 1984 and 1985, the National Aeronautics and Space Administration (NASA) coordinated a major international scientific review, and a powerful case for international action was made. The review pointed out that CFCs in the atmosphere had doubled between 1975 and 1985, and it projected a 9 percent depletion of stratospheric ozone by 2050 if 1980 use rates of CFCs continued. Additional skin cancers from the resulting increase in ultraviolet radiation were estimated. The framework convention, the Vienna Convention for the Protection of the Ozone Layer, followed promptly in 1985.

This framework convention merely called on governments to take "appropriate measures." It also took two steps that are now common features of the treaty world. It established a "Conference of the Parties" to the convention consisting of all countries that had joined the convention. And it established a UN secretariat to service the Conference on the Parties. These secretariats are of great importance. They can commission studies, consolidate research results, develop ideas for protocols and early drafts of them, and generally provide ongoing expertise and frame the agenda for the Conference of the Parties. The Conference of the Parties itself becomes the body empowered to draft proposed amendments to the Vienna Convention and proposed protocols implementing it.

The more serious ozone negotiations were those leading to the 1987 Montreal Protocol. Two big hurdles had to be overcome. The United States and others in the "lead states coalition" advocated, first, a freeze on CFC production and, second, a 95 percent phase-out of their production over 10 to 14 years. These measures were resisted strongly by the chemical manufacturers, represented in the United States by the 50-member Alliance for a Responsible CFC Policy. That was the first stumbling block.

The other was Europe. Europe seems ahead of the United States today on climate protection and other international environmental issues, but that was not true in earlier periods. On ozone protection, most major European governments tended to adopt entirely the position advocated by their national companies.

How was this situation turned around? First, the U.S. State Department made the ozone issue a true priority and lobbied more than 60 other governments intensively, an effort vigorously promoted by U.S. ambassador Richard Benedick. Second, the single biggest manufacturer, DuPont, announced in 1986 that it could develop CFC substitutes within five years. But DuPont was reluctant to initiate production of these substitutes unless strong international regulation created a market for them by phasing out CFCs. Others in industry understood that they would be better off with international action than with further unilateral U.S. action, which was also a strong possibility. As a result, unified industry opposition crumbled. Third, UNEP's executive director, Mostafa Tolba, forcefully pushed for action, putting both his and the UN's weight and credibility on the line. Strong personal leadership from outstanding individuals has proven essential in forging many global agreements. Fourth, a major "focusing event" occurred when the ozone hole was discovered over Antarctica. And, finally, the United States, the Europeans, and other governments showed a willingness to compromise. In the end the Montreal Protocol required that the industrial countries reduce their CFC production by 50 percent below 1986 levels by 1999.

> In the end the **Montreal Protocol** required that the industrial countries reduce their CFC production by 50 percent below 1986 levels by 1999.

Though they are often overlapping and even blended together in practice, a series of logically sequential steps are involved in the process of moving from the point where key governments realize that international action is required (agenda setting) to the point of having an agreement ready for signing and ratification by governments:

- *Coalition building.* The "lead states" must reach out to "supporting states," which will speak in favor of action, and to "swing states" which need minor concessions or incentives to join the coalition.

- *Policy formulation and selection.* The emerging coalition must decide on the policy and regulatory approach it prefers from among the various options.

- *Formal negotiations.* The coalition members must often find ways to overcome "veto states." Typically, in international environmental negotiations there are countries whose participation is so essential to the success of the effort that they have the power to block effective international action. If such countries are prepared to use their de facto veto power, they must be accommodated in some way that secures their participation and, it is hoped, in a way that does not undermine the integrity of the emerging regime.

In the case of the ozone treaty process, including the Montreal Protocol and its subsequent amendments, negotiators and other participants successfully navigated these steps in ways that are instructive on how the policy process works more generally. First and most obviously, intense intergovernmental bargaining and negotiation are involved. In the ozone case, two potential veto coalitions—several major European countries and several large developing countries—were won over, the Europeans by compromising initially on the CFC phase-down requirements and the developing countries by creating a special international fund to support their transition from ozone-depleting substances and by postponing for a decade the application to them of phase-down requirements.

These and other multilateral negotiations can only be understood as an outgrowth of what has been called the "two-level game," a process in which international decisions are reached as a result of the interaction of international politics and national politics. Domestic economic and political factors powerfully influence and often determine positions taken by governments in international negotiations. It is easy to see why. Domestic acceptance and ratification of the agreement and its conscientious implementation are both essential.

Finally, the ozone treaty process brings out clearly the importance of business corporations and economic interests as actors in shaping the outcome of international negotiations. Political analysts Peter Newell and David Levy examined the role of corporations in the United States and Europe and concluded that "government negotiating positions in Europe and the United States have tended to track the stances of major industries active on key issues, such that the achievement of global environmental accords is impossible if important economic sectors are unified in opposition."[2] Political scientist Gareth Porter and his coauthors note that "corporations have worked to weaken several global environmental regimes, including ozone protection, climate change, whaling, the international toxic waste trade, and fisheries."[3] But they also note corporations are not monolithic, and that some may benefit from international requirements, even firms within the same industry. And, indeed, getting tough ozone protection agreements was much aided by the switch noted earlier in the position of DuPont.

Formal Adoption

The third stage in the treaty-making process is the formal adoption stage. As discussed in an earlier section (International Law and Collective Action), conventions and protocols are first signed but do not "enter into force" until they are ratified by a specified number of countries or, sometimes, countries representing a specified share of the problem or its solution. The ratification process is by no means a sure thing. The United States has one of the worst records in the world when it comes to adoption of international environmental agreements, even those like the Kyoto Protocol that it heavily shaped and signed. International politics continue into this stage. Although debates about the language of an agreement are typically off limits at this point in the process, proponents of an agreement can offer various inducements to other countries to join, while opponents have been known to offer inducements to the contrary. Europe, for example, lobbied Russia to join the Kyoto Protocol, and it is widely believed that the United States discouraged this move, unsuccessfully.

Implementation, Monitoring, Assessment, and Strengthening

In this final stage of the convention/protocol process the ozone convention process is again instructive. Driven by further science and by focusing events like the ozone hole over Antarctica, the Ozone Protection Conference of the Parties has responded repeatedly to strengthen the regime. As Gareth Porter and his colleagues have observed, the Montreal Protocol is the best example so far of a regime that has been continually strengthened in response to new scientific evidence and technological changes. As a result, if developing nations reduce their emissions as expected, scientists are now forecasting the recovery of the ozone layer by around 2050, though the process of recovery has hardly begun.

The Montreal Protocol is by almost all accounts the most successful international environmental regime. Diplomats, corporations, scientists, and environmental leaders have succeeded in sharply reducing the release of ozone-depleting substances. It is now possible to envision recovery of Earth's ozone shield—a remarkable accomplishment.

Treaty Regimes and the Other Major Global Environmental Threats

What of the other nine global challenges reviewed in chapter 2? What treaty regimes and other approaches have been developed to meet these challenges? Here in brief is what the international community has done in each case.

1. *Acid rain and regional air pollution.* The Convention on Long-Range Transboundary Air Pollution, a regional agreement involving Europe, regulates emissions of both sulfur and nitrogen oxides. Some countries, including the United States, have their own domestic regulations, and the United States and Canada have an important bilateral air quality agreement. These efforts are gradually succeeding, but the recovery of acidified water bodies has been slow. See www.unece.org/env/lrtap.

2. *Climate disruption.* The Earth Summit at Rio was the site of the signing of the Framework Convention on Climate Change of 1992, and funding to assist the developing world is available under the Global Environment Facility (GEF). The now-famous 1997 Kyoto Protocol is an agreement within the framework of this convention. The Kyoto Protocol entered into force in 2005, even without U.S. participation, thanks to Russian ratification in 2004. The Kyoto Protocol sets specific targets and timetables for the reduction of climate-altering gases in industrial countries. Whether the Kyoto Protocol will generate success like the Montreal Protocol is discussed later in this chapter. Meanwhile, global carbon dioxide emissions and the buildup of CO_2 in the atmosphere have continued to climb steadily since the 1992 Earth Summit. See www.unfccc.int and www.ipcc.ch.

3. *Deforestation.* No convention has yet been adopted addressing world forests or deforestation, but nonbinding principles to guide the sustainable management of forests were agreed to at the Rio Earth

Summit. They were followed by an impressive international effort led by environmental organizations and private foundations to promote the certification and ecolabeling of forest products when those products are derived from sustainable forest management based on these principles. There has also been a substantial increase in development assistance and NGO activity to protect tropical forests. These efforts have not yet appreciably slowed deforestation in the tropics. See www.iisd.ca/vol13.

4. *Land degradation and desertification.* Here, principally two things have happened: (1) following a commitment at the Rio Earth Summit, the international community agreed in 1994 to the Convention to Combat Desertification, and (2) efforts have since been made to increase the volume of development aid targeted to this problem. GEF coverage was recently extended to desertification. This convention, like those for biodiversity and climate, contains requirements that participating governments develop their own plans of action focused on the issue. The success of the desertification convention depends critically on major international financial support, which has not been forthcoming. See www.unccd.int.

5. *Freshwater degradation and shortages.* The Convention on the Non-navigable Uses of International Watercourses has been negotiated but has not gone into effect, and it may never succeed unless political support picks up. A number of regional agreements now address the environmental aspects of watershed management, but, generally, there is little international protection of freshwater resources. Funding for protection of international waterways is one of the funding windows under the GEF. See www.un.org/law/ilc/.

6. *Marine fisheries decline.* A host of international agreements, including the UN Convention on the Law of the Sea, now cover ocean pollution, overfishing, whaling, and other issues. International environmental law is arguably more developed in the oceans area than any other, as one might expect, and the regimes addressing marine pollution, ocean dumping, and whaling have had considerable success. The same cannot be said for international protection of marine fisheries, where short-term economic interests routinely trump good science. See www.fao.org/fi/default.asp and www.un.org/ depts/los/index.htm.

7. *Toxic pollutants.* The Basel Convention now regulates the international toxic wastes trade, and the Stockholm Convention on Persistent Organic Pollutants (POPs), promoting the phaseout of 12 highly dangerous chemicals, was signed in 2001 and entered into force in 2004. While most of these substances were already heavily regulated, the POPs convention provides a framework for the regulation of other chemicals in the future. The 1998 Rotterdam Convention calls for "prior informed consent" for trade in pesticides and industrial chemicals, as do the 1985 Food and Agriculture Organization of the United Nations (FAO) Code of Conduct on the Distribution and Use of Pesticides and the 1987 London Guidelines for the Exchange of Information on Chemicals in International Trade. The European acid rain agreement now also addresses airborne emissions of various toxic chemicals. UNEP coordinates an online directory of toxic chemicals. See www. basel.int, www.pops. int, and www.pic.int.

8. *Loss of biological diversity.* The Convention on Biological Diversity was signed at the Rio Earth Summit in 1992. Funding to support biodiversity conservation is provided under the GEF. As with forest protection, NGOs and the development assistance community have increased cooperation to protect biodiversity. Many other conventions address narrower issues of wildlife and habitat protection. (See chap. 3.) There is little evidence that the Biodiversity Convention is doing much to curb the loss of species or ecosystem services. See www.biodiv.org.

9. *Excess nitrogen.* No explicit treaties have been concluded on nitrogen pollution, and there are no effective international controls on the overall problem. Various sources of nitrogen to the environment are covered in FAO voluntary guidelines for the handling and use of agricultural chemicals. The 1988 European Nitrogen Oxides Protocol regulates the amount of nitrogen oxides that can be emitted into the atmosphere. See www.unece.org/env.lrtap.

How should one appraise these efforts of the international community? Opinions differ both on the best way to measure regime effectiveness and on the magnitude of the accomplishment represented by these treaties and related aspects of international environmental law.

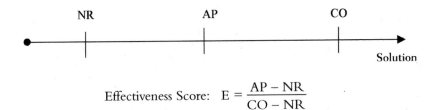

$$\text{Effectiveness Score:} \quad E = \frac{AP - NR}{CO - NR}$$

Figure 4.3

On measuring regime effectiveness, one simple conceptual framework starts with three levels of accomplishment: (1) what the situation would have been without the regime, sometimes referred to as the "no-regime counterfactual" (NR); (2) the actual performance obtained under the international regime (AP); and (3) the best result that could be accomplished, the "collective optimum" (CO). For example, perhaps the CO for ozone protection is 95 percent reduction in releases of ozone-depleting substances. The difference between NR and AP is a measure of "whether regimes matter." The difference between AP and CO tells us the degree to which a particular problem is "solved" under the regime. These two measures can be combined as shown in the figure here.

The effectiveness score gives us an expression of the gains actually achieved by the regime as a percentage of the gains needed to solve the problem.[4]

Many international lawyers and political scientists are impressed by what has been achieved (i.e., the move from NR to AP). They tend to look at what has been built from a base of near zero. One political scientist put the matter as follows: "Before [1972], national leaders were by and large unfamiliar with environmental issues; scientific understanding was rudimentary; and there were few national or international institutions available for promoting environmental protection. Over the last thirty years, however, the environment has become firmly established on the international diplomatic agenda, and, through regime formation, binding rules have been developed for most human activities affecting environmental quality. Almost all areas of human economic activity are now subject to at least one international environmental accord, and most countries are bound by a number of international environmental commitments. One feature of international environmental governance is particularly striking: national governments have become increasingly aware of the complexity of the threats to the world's ecosystems and of the need for more comprehensive and collective responses. Accordingly, the substance of regional and international legal arrangements on the environment has begun to reflect this awareness. Environmental governance—the ever-expanding network of legal obligations and formal institutions influencing states' environmental policies—has evolved principally through the development of better scientific understanding about the behavior of the physical environment combined with a growing appreciation of the role that international institutions can play. These regulations and institutions have contributed to a structural change in the world economy and to the development of markets for clean technology."[5]

And a leading law treatise offers a similarly positive assessment: "[I]t must be accepted that the main part of international environmental law comprises the treaty regimes. . . . The impact of these, both on customary law and in themselves, should not be underestimated. . . . Most of the major global agreements, including the Rio treaties and the 1982 Law of the Sea, enjoy very wide participation, are in force, and have begun to exert significant influence on international environmental law and practice."[6]

A different perspective comes into view, however, if one asks whether international environmental law is actually succeeding in reversing the disturbing global environmental trends reviewed in chapter 2 (i.e., how close is AP to CO?). Applying this standard, one student of international environmental affairs recently provided the following assessment: "Despite all the effort, the disturbing trends noticed twenty years ago continue essentially unabated, ozone depletion being a notable exception. The problems are more deeply entrenched, and time is now short. Judging from this fact, as well as the analysis of particular treaty regimes affecting specific issues such as climate and biodiversity, it is a fair if unfortunate conclusion that this first effort at global environmental governance has largely failed. The international community has not acted decisively to reverse the trends, and the results of twenty years of international environmental negotiations are deeply disappointing. It is not that what has been agreed upon, for example, in the framework conventions on climate, desertification, biodiversity or the Law of the Sea is wrong or useless. Those conventions have raised awareness, provided frameworks for action, and stimulated useful national planning exercises. But the bottom line is that these treaties and their associated agreements and protocols do not drive the changes that are needed.

In general, the issue with these treaties is not weak enforcement or non-compliance; the issue is weak treaties.

"Thus far, the climate convention is not protecting climate, the biodiversity convention is not protecting biodiversity, the desertification convention is not preventing desertification, and even the older and stronger Convention on the Law of the Sea is not protecting fisheries. Nor are they poised to do so. The same can be said for the extensive international discussions on world forests, which never have reached the point of a convention."[7]

As we saw in chapter 2, most of the major global environmental threats have not been met effectively, and in most areas conditions are projected to worsen. What accounts for the inability of treaties and international environmental law to have dealt more successfully with these challenges? Environmental policy analyst David Leonard Downie has prepared a catalogue of impediments to effective environmental regimes. He identifies four categories of factors: (1) systemic obstacles, (2) procedural obstacles, (3) lack of necessary and sufficient conditions, and (4) characteristics of international environmental issues.[8]

1. Systemic obstacles

   • Effective cooperation among assertive nation-states in the international political system is inherently difficult. The structure of an international system of autonomous nations meshes poorly with the nature of large-scale environmental issues, which defy national boundaries and are linked geographically and temporally in complicated ways.

   • International law gives countries sovereign legal authority within their borders, but environmental progress requires that they relinquish the freedom of action that sovereignty holds out.

2. Procedural obstacles

   • Since countries can choose to join or not join international agreements, important countries can typically change agreements to fit their interests, resulting in lowest common denominator agreements.

   • Reaching international agreement takes time and can be torturously slow, yet the problems do not wait on their solutions.

3. Lack of necessary conditions

- Critical preconditions, such as a high level of public concern and administrative skills and capacities within governments, are frequently lacking.

4. Characteristics of international environmental issues

- Global environmental issues are complex, difficult to understand, and full of uncertainties.

- These global issues also pose constraints to economic laissez-faire, and addressing these issues can have significant economic costs, particularly to some firms and economic sectors.

- Solutions to global environmental problems have unequal distributions of costs and benefits among nations.

- Global environmental threats are typically chronic threats, slow in unfolding, whereas political leaders and corporate CEOs have short time horizons.

Some observers, such as Robert C. Paehlke, have stressed another pattern: "[S]pecific problems—especially those with technical solutions of modest economic costs—have relatively good prospects of success through the treaty route [but] the broader the problem and the more important the economic implications, the more thorough the failure of treaty-based environmental initiatives so far."[9]

Jennifer Clapp has noted that in an increasingly globalized economy environmental problems can "morph" or evolve easily into new ones, for example, as companies skillfully find ways around treaty restrictions.[10]

With so many impediments to effective international action on the environmental front, it is not difficult to see why progress has been slow. Such impediments should not be viewed fatalistically; they should be seen as pointing to corrective actions that are needed. We take that topic up in chapter 6 when we look at needed reforms.

Will Climate Protection Be the Next Success?

With the Kyoto Protocol's entry into force in 2005, it is fair to ask whether it will be the next Montreal Protocol, driving action to protect climate as the Montreal Protocol drove action to protect the ozone layer. Put more broadly, is the climate treaty regime now poised at last for major impact?

Our answer to this second question is a highly qualified yes. At this writing, in 2005, the international community seems finally to have come to believe in what it said it believed in 13 years earlier when it adopted the UN Framework Convention on Climate Change; namely, climate change is a serious problem requiring major reductions in greenhouse gas emissions.* All the industrial countries except the United States and Australia have ratified the Kyoto Protocol and are making efforts to comply. The European Union and numerous individual countries have carbon-trading schemes in place, and these and other measures are pushing major corporations to adopt significant carbon reduction programs. Europe is also looking beyond the current Kyoto Protocol terms to the "second commitment period" after 2012, where they are seeking much deeper cuts in greenhouse gas emissions. The United Kingdom has put in place a national policy of reducing its emissions by 60 percent by midcentury. Even in the United States scores of major corporations, over 180 cities, and many states have announced plans for complying with Kyoto-type goals. The northeastern states are developing a regional cap-and-trade program to reduce emissions from power plants, and California is showing leadership again in regulating the automobile industry, this time focusing on its greenhouse gas emissions. In the most far-reaching step yet, Governor Arnold Schwarzenegger of California has called for an 80 percent cut in the state's greenhouse gas emissions by 2050.

These positive developments leave many questions unanswered, however. It is not clear that even Europe and Japan will actually meet Kyoto's requirements for the 2008–2012 period, and it is abundantly clear that the world's largest climate polluter, the United States, will not come close to meeting the Kyoto targets set for it in an agreement it signed but never ratified. Moreover, what will happen in the post-2012 period is undetermined. In 2005 international negotiations on post-2012 had hardly begun.

The truly bad news is that it seems unlikely that the international community will achieve the overriding objective of the climate treaty—to forestall dangerous anthropogenic interference with the global climate system. Opinions on what is "dangerous" differ, as one would expect, but given the late start in regulating these gases in virtually all countries, the absence of

---

*There are four paths to reduced industrial CO_2 emissions: energy efficiency, nonfossil energy, lighter hydrocarbons (e.g. natural gas), and carbon capture and storage.

positive leadership from the United States over a long period, the prolonged failure to have found a way of engaging the developing world (China is the world's number two greenhouse gas polluter), the huge increases in fossil fuel use and carbon emissions projected in all "business as usual" models of the world economy, and the severe environmental and economic impacts of atmospheric greenhouse gas concentrations that now seem highly likely to eventuate, it is doubtful that we will be able one day to look back on the climate treaty and pronounce it a success."[11]

Annex: A Timeline of Major International Environmental Agreements

1972   United Nations Conference on the Human Environment (UNCHE), Stockholm
Stockholm Declaration adopted.

1973   United Nations Environment Programme (UNEP) created

1973   Convention on International Trade in Endangered Species (CITES)
Entered into force 1975.

1979   Convention on Long Range Transboundary Air Pollution (CLRTAP)
Entered into force 1983.

1982   United Nations Convention on the Law of the Sea (UNCLOS)
Entered into force 1994.

1985   Vienna Convention for the Protection of the Ozone Layer
Entered into force 1988.

1987   Montreal Protocol on Substances that Deplete the Ozone Layer
Entered into force 1989.

1987   World Commission on Environment and Development (WCED)
Publication of the Brundtland Report.

1989   Basel Convention on the Control of Transboundary Movements of Hazardous Wastes and Their Disposal
Entered into force 1992.

1991   Establishment of the Global Environmental Facility (GEF)

1992   United Nations Conference on Environment and Development (UNCED)
Rio de Janeiro (The Earth Summit)
Rio Declaration adopted.
Agenda 21 adopted.

1992   United Nations Framework Convention on Climate Change (UNFCCC)
Entered into force 1994.

1992   United Nations Commission on Sustainable Development (CSD) created.

1992   United Nations Convention on Biological Diversity
Entered into force 1993.

1994   International Convention to Combat Desertification
Entered into force 1996.

1997   Kyoto Protocol on Climate Change adopted
Entered into force 2005.

1998   Rotterdam Convention on the Prior Informed Consent Procedure for Certain Hazardous Chemicals and Pesticides in International Trade
Entered into force 2004.

2000   Cartagena Protocol on Biosafety adopted.
Entered into force 2003.

2001   Stockholm Convention for the Elimination of the Persistent Organic Pollutants (POPs) adopted.
Entered into force 2004.

2002   World Summit on Sustainable Development (WSSD) held in Johannesburg
Johannesburg Declaration adopted.
Johannesburg Plan of Implementation adopted.

V

Key Actors, Expanding Roles: The United Nations, International Organizations, and Civil Society

WE HAVE SEEN THAT TODAY'S GLOBAL ENVIRONMENTAL GOVERNANCE HAS BEEN built in close concert with the United Nations, other intergovernmental organizations such as the World Bank, and what has come to be called "civil society," a term that comprises both the private for-profit business sector and the not-for-profit nongovernmental organizations (NGOs). We saw all these actors playing large roles in the drama from Stockholm to Johannesburg and, close-up, in the story of the protection of the ozone layer. While governments themselves are the primary players, and thus must take responsibility for successes and failures, the international organizations governments have created and the civil society organizations outside government have wielded powerful influence every step of the way. In this chapter we look in more detail at the way these actors are organized, their motivations, and the roles they have played to date.

The United Nations System

From the early days of the ill-fated League of Nations to the present, governments have created a complex and sometimes bewildering array of intergovernmental organizations to meet the needs of an increasingly integrated and complex world. They promote a variety of widely shared objectives—peace and security, health and education, development and livelihoods, trade and economic stability, human rights, and, recently, environmental protection, to mention but a few.

Most prominent in this world of intergovernmental organizations is what has come to be called the United Nations system. (The organizational diagram provided by the United Nations—presented here—is well known

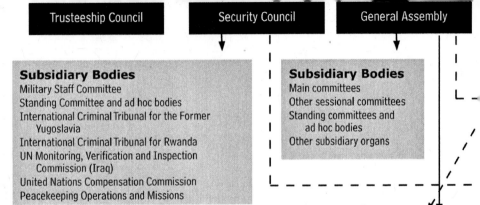

Trusteeship Council	Security Council	General Assembly

Subsidiary Bodies
Military Staff Committee
Standing Committee and ad hoc bodies
International Criminal Tribunal for the Former
    Yugoslavia
International Criminal Tribunal for Rwanda
UN Monitoring, Verification and Inspection
    Commission (Iraq)
United Nations Compensation Commission
Peacekeeping Operations and Missions

Subsidiary Bodies
Main committees
Other sessional committees
Standing committees and
    ad hoc bodies
Other subsidiary organs

Programmes and Funds

UNCTAD United Nations
Conference on Trade and
Development
   ITC International Trade Centre
   (UNCTAD/WTO)
UNDCP United Nations Drug
Control Programme[1]
UNEP United Nations
Environment Programme
UNICEF United Nations
Children's Fund

UNDP United Nations
Development Programme
   UNIFEM United Nations
   Development Fund for Women
   UNV United Nations
   Volunteers
   UNCDF United Nations
   Capital Development Fund
UNFPA United Nations
Population Fund

UNHCR Office of the United
Nations High Commissioner for
Refugees
WFP World Food Programme
UNRWA[2] United Nations Relief
and Works Agency for Palestine
Refugees in the Near East
UN–HABITAT United
Nations Human Settlements
Programme (UNHSP)

Research and Training Institutes

UNICRI United Nations
Interregional Crime and Justice
Research Institute
UNITAR United Nations
Institute for Training and
Research

UNRISD United Nations
Research Institute for Social
Development
UNIDIR[2] United Nations
Institute for Disarmament
Research

INSTRAW International
Research and Training Institute
for the Advancement of Women

Other UN Entities

OHCHR Office of the
United Nations High
Commissioner for
Human Rights

UNOPS United
Nations Office for
Project Services

UNU United Nations
University
UNSSC United
Nations System Staff
College

UNAIDS Joint United
Nations Programme on
HIV/AIDS

NOTES: Solid lines from a Principal Organ indicate a direct reporting relationship; dashes indicate a non-subsidiary relationship. [1]The UN Drug Control Programme is part of the UN Office on Drugs and Crime. [2]UNRWA and UNIDIR report only to the GA. [3]The World Trade Organization and World Tourism Organization use the same acronym. [4]IAEA reports to the Security Council and the General Assembly (GA). [5]The CTBTO Prep.Com and OPCW report to the GA. [6]Specialized agencies are autonomous organizations working with the UN and each other through the coordinating machinery of the ECOSOC at the intergovernmental level, and through the Chief Executives Board for coordination (CEB) at the inter-secretariat level.

Figure 5.1   The United Nations System, Principal Organs

Economic and Social Council	International Court of Justice	Secretariat
↓	↓	↓

Functional Commissions

Commissions on:
- Human Rights
- Narcotic Drugs
- Crime Prevention and Criminal Justice
- Science and Technology for Development
- Sustainable Development
- Status of Women
- Population and Development

Commission for Social Development

Statistical Commission

Regional Commissions

Economic Commission for Africa (ECA)

Economic Commission for Europe (ECE)

Economic Commission for Latin America and the Caribbean (ECLAC)

Economic and Social Commission for Asia and the Pacific (ESCAP)

Economic and Social Commission for Western Asia (ESCWA)

Other Bodies

Permanent Forum on Indigenous Issues (PFII)

United Nations Forum on Forests

Sessional and standing committees

Expert, ad hoc and related bodies

Related Organizations

WTO[3] World Trade Organization

IAEA[4] International Atomic Energy Agency

CTBTO PREP.COM[5] PrepCom for the Nuclear-Test-Ban-Treaty Organization

OPCW[5] Organization for the Prohibition of Chemical Weapons

Specialized Agencies[6]

ILO International Labour Organization

FAO Food and Agriculture Organization of the United Nations

UNESCO United Nations Educational, Scientific and Cultural Organization

WHO World Health Organization

WORLD BANK GROUP

IBRD International Bank for Reconstruction and Development

IDA International Development Association

IFC International Finance Corporation

MIGA Multilateral Investment Guarantee Agency

ICSID International Centre for Settlement of Investment Disputes

IMF International Monetary Fund

ICAO International Civil Aviation Organization

IMO International Maritime Organization

ITU International Telecommunication Union

UPU Universal Postal Union

WMO World Meterological Organization

WIPO World Intellectual Property Organization

IFAD International Fund for Agricultural Development

UNIDO United Nations Industrial Development Organization

WTO[3] World Tourism Organization

Departments and Offices

OSG Office of the Secretary-General

OIOS Office of Internal Oversight Services

OLA Office of Legal Affairs

DPA Department of Political Affairs

DDA Department for Disarmament Affairs

DPKO Department of Peace-keeping Operations

OCHA Office for the Coordination of Humanitarian Affairs

DESA Department of Economic and Social Affairs

DGACM Department for General Assembly and Conference Management

DPI Department of Public Information

DM Department of Management

OHRLLS Office of the High Representative for the Least Developed Countries, Landlocked Developing Countries and Small Island Developing States

UNSECOORD Office of the United Nations Security Coordinator

UNODC United Nations Office on Drugs and Crime

☙

UNOG UN Office at Geneva

UNOV UN Office at Vienna

UNON UN Office at Nairobi

Published by the UN Department of Public Information
DPI/2342—March 2004

for being unhelpful.) The best way to make the United Nations system intelligible is to imagine three concentric circles. In the center circle is the United Nations proper, where the principal institutions are the General Assembly, the Security Council, and the Economic and Social Council (ECOSOC).* The Secretariat, led by the Secretary-General of the United Nations, provides staff and support services to the intergovernmental deliberations carried out in the three principal organs. The organs in this innermost circle are what most people think of as the United Nations, and it is this sphere that is most important for global environmental governance.

> The Secretariat, led by the Secretary-General of the United Nations, provides staff and support services to the intergovernmental deliberations carried out in the three principal organs. The organs in this innermost circle are what most people think of as the **United Nations,** and it is this sphere that is most important for global environmental governance.

Arrayed loosely under the General Assembly and ECOSOC are a series of UN agencies and entities that are of most concern to us. Here we find the UN Environment Programme (UNEP), the UN Development Programme (UNDP), the UN Population Fund (UNFPA), the UN Children's Fund (UNICEF), the World Food Programme (WFP), the UN High Commissioners for Refugees and for Human Rights (UNHCR and UNHCHR), the regional economic commissions of the United Nations, and many others. These are all actual agencies with their own staffs and programs. Separate but also reporting to ECOSOC are a series of intergovernmental deliberative bodies staffed by the Secretariat. Most important for our purposes is the Commission on Sustainable Development (CSD), created after the Rio Earth Summit.

Within the UN proper, these bodies and agencies carry out two distinct functions: normative and operational. UNEP, for example, is primarily a normative agency; that is, it is focused on providing information, raising awareness, promoting environmental principles and norms, and stimulating the development and implementation of hard and soft law. In its nor-

*The Trusteeship Council is largely defunct, and the International Court of Justice is still finding its way in the world. The Security Council is far and away the most powerful part of the United Nations, but it has rarely dipped into our issues even to explore the links between peace and security and environmental stresses.

mative work UNEP's primary achievement has been the rapid expansion of international environmental law. The UN's Economic Commission for Europe has also done extensive normative work in the environmental area—for example, leading in European efforts to regulate acid rain. UNDP, on the other hand, is an operational agency focusing on carrying out development assistance operations in poorer countries. UNEP's focus is on the world, North and South, and its primary mandate has become to provide the leadership, norms, and rules of the road for protecting the global environment. UNDP, on the other hand, focuses on the developing world and its job is to use its development assistance resources wisely for the maximum benefit of the poorer countries it serves. These lines are not hard and fast. UNDP sometimes addresses normative issues, such as international policies needed to achieve sustainable human development, and UNEP carries out modest operational activities, for example, capacity building in developing country environmental programs. Still, the normative–operational distinction is critical to keep in mind.

Within the UN proper, these bodies and agencies carry out two distinct functions: normative and operational. UNEP, for example, is primarily a normative agency; that is, it is focused on providing information, raising awareness, promoting environmental principles and norms, and stimulating the development and implementation of hard and soft law.

UNEP carries out modest operational activities, for example, capacity building in developing country environmental programs.

Within this framework, let us examine the principal UN entities relevant to the global environment. There are three entities, or groups of entities, of primary interest, and they are all on the normative side.

- *UNEP.* Despite its small size and its location in Nairobi, Kenya, away from the main UN centers, UNEP, as we have seen, has been the spark plug that fired the development of modern global environmental governance. But it has lacked the mandate, size, authority, and resources to do the job expected of the world's environmental leader at the international level.

- *The Convention Conferences of the Parties (COPs) and Secretariats.* As with the ozone convention, most of the major treaty regimes have their own COPs, the group of countries that have ratified the convention in question and are parties to it. These COPs meet on a regular basis and, by treaty, are responsible for the operation of the convention. They monitor its progress and propose protocols and treaty amendments to governments. Each COP is typically serviced and staffed by a secretariat comprised of UN employees. UNEP provides secretariat services for some conventions, but others are independent of UNEP and located in various places—the climate and desertification convention secretariats are in Bonn, Germany; the ozone convention secretariat is in Montreal, and so on. A fair generalization is that the various convention COPs and their secretariats have grown in independence, importance, and stature, and because many of the most important are independent of UNEP, they have tended to drain funding, support, and influence away from UNEP.

- *The Commission on Sustainable Development.* As we saw in chapter 3, the CSD is an intergovernmental forum created by the UN General Assembly to monitor the implementation of *Agenda 21* and the Rio Earth Summit. It meets annually at UN headquarters in New York. Like ECOSOC itself, the CSD has been criticized often for being little more than a "talk shop," long on speech-making but short on stimulating action. Though its annual meetings have certainly advanced the understanding of key issues and environment–development linkages among UN member states, some observers believe it is now largely a distraction that should be abolished.

In addition to its normative work, the UN proper carries out extensive operational activities, providing both development assistance and humanitarian relief around the world. Although only UNDP among the UN's development agencies has made environment a significant part of its mandate, other UN funds and programs also have relevance for environmental prospects in developing countries, including especially UNFPA, UNICEF, WFP, and the UN Human Settlements Programme (UN-HABITAT). While the work of the UN's development-oriented funds and programs can and has helped to promote sustainable development and provided capacity-building assistance in the developing world, of greater importance for the global environment has been the UN's normative work and especially its sponsorship of international environmental law. We take up the issue of development assistance and the environment in the section that follows.

In the next concentric circle beyond the innermost one we find what are called the specialized agencies of the United Nations. The most relevant for the environment are UN Educational, Scientific, and Cultural Organization (UNESCO), Food and Agriculture Organization (FAO), World Health Organization (WHO), World Meteorological Organization (WMO), and the UN Industrial Development Organization (UNIDO). In many ways each of these agencies is an equal to the United Nations proper. Most of the specialized agencies predated the creation of the United Nations in 1945; they have their own charters and general assemblies, which select their own secretaries-general, some of whom view the UN Secretary-General as only *primus inter pares* with them. The specialized agencies also have their own separate funding and budgets, typically assessed contributions from member countries. They are linked to the UN proper by "relationship agreements" only, and are not under the UN General Assembly or the UN Secretary-General.

The specialized agencies carry out both normative and operational functions, and a modest portion of their work is relevant to the environment. UNESCO, for example, sponsors the World Heritage Convention, which seeks to protect natural and cultural sites of great international importance; the FAO provides extensive normative leadership and some technical assistance on agriculture and forestry; and WHO's focus on international public health issues sometimes touches on environmental health concerns.

In the outermost circle we find the Bretton Woods Institutions—the World Bank and the International Monetary Fund (IMF)—which are nominally part of the UN System but which in practical and legal terms are even more independent of the UN proper than the specialized agencies. And beyond the concentric circles, outside the UN System, is the World Trade Organization (WTO). The World Bank and the WTO are discussed in the two sections that follow.

In sum, the UN system is a significant provider of international development assistance to the poorer countries. But where the United Nations has been indispensable for the environment is in its normative role as essentially the sole provider of the leadership and platform giving rise to the principles, programs of action, and treaty regimes that constitute the main body of today's environmental governance at the international level. This singular accomplishment is often overlooked amidst the often-strident criticism of the United Nations in other fields.

Development Assistance and the Environment

The developing countries are the sites of some of today's most serious environmental deterioration. Deforestation, biodiversity loss, desertification, and local air pollution are most acute there. Acid rain is declining in Europe and North America but increasing in Asia. Developing country citizens have experienced some of the worst exposure to toxic chemicals, and while the industrial countries are still the major emitters of climate-changing greenhouse

---

SOUNDINGS • *Knight-Ridder News*

IN CHINA'S DASH TO DEVELOP, ENVIRONMENT SUFFERS SEVERELY

HUAXI, CHINA, JULY 25, 2005—China's environmental woes are so large that they've begun to generate social instability.

Choking on vile air, sickened by toxic water, citizens in some corners of this vast nation are rising up to protest the high environmental cost of China's economic boom.

In one recent incident, villagers in this hilly coastal region grew so exasperated by contamination from nearby chemical plants that they overturned and smashed dozens of vehicles and beat up police officers who arrived to quell what was essentially an environmental riot.

"We had to do it. We can't grow our vegetables here anymore," said Li Sanye, a 60-year-old farmer. "Young women are giving birth to stillborn babies."

Across China, entire rivers run foul or have dried up altogether. Nearly a third of cities don't treat their sewage, flushing it into waterways. Some 300 million of China's 1.3 billion people drink water that is too contaminated to be consumed safely. In rural China, sooty air depresses crop yields, and deserts quickly encroaches on grasslands to the west. Filth and grime cover all but a few corners of the country.

China's central government isn't sitting still. It's enacting fuel-efficiency requirements for cars and shutting down mammoth dam-building and other projects. By some accounts, it now has world-class laws on environmental protection.

Yet provincial and local officials, who feel pressure for economic growth, often shield polluters and ignore environmental laws.

gases, emissions from developing regions, especially China and India, are growing rapidly. By 2015, for example, greenhouse gas emissions from the transportation sector in the developing world could equal or exceed those of the industrial countries. The developing world is also home to almost 80 percent of the world's people, and the future site of major economic growth. A number of questions come to the fore:

- Will developing world growth be consistent with the principles of sustainable development? Will the developing countries cooperate and, where appropriate, lead in realizing the goals of the major treaty regimes? How will developing country governments balance and integrate their developmental and environmental objectives?

- Will the international development assistance agencies, and particularly the largest and most influential of these agencies, the World Bank, be forces for the integration of environmental concerns into development strategies and projects, or will they support traditional development in their policy advocacy and project planning? Will the development assistance community fully support the goals of environmental treaties and work with developing countries to integrate treaty goals into national development strategies and programs?

- What should be fair burden-sharing between North and South regarding the costs and risks involved in the developing world committing to sustainable development and protection of the global environment?

As our history from Stockholm to Johannesburg shows, these questions have surfaced repeatedly in international conferences and negotiations. Much depends on how they are answered, and much of the answer would seem to depend on whether the richer industrial countries set the right examples in their own development and consumption patterns and pursue supportive policies in aid, trade, investment, and management of the developing world's international indebtedness.

Official development assistance (ODA) from the Organization for Economic Cooperation and Development (OECD) countries to the poorer ones is about $60 billion—too small to have a huge impact in and of itself. By comparison, foreign direct investment in the developing world is several times ODA. But this comparison can be misleading. The development assistance community's role is bigger than it appears, for several reasons. Development

> **Development assistance**
> *(as well as forgiveness of
> international indebtedness) is
> often made conditional on policy
> changes in developing countries;
> it is also often focused
> "upstream" in the planning
> process rather than downstream
> at the level of on-the-ground
> projects.*

assistance (as well as forgiveness of international indebtedness) is often made conditional on policy changes in developing countries; it is also often focused "upstream" in the planning process rather than downstream at the level of on-the-ground projects, and it thus can have greater leverage; and by providing assistance through loans that vary from commercial to concessional, the World Bank can further leverage its resources. (The World Bank's loans that are below market rates contain a "gift" element that is included in the calculation of ODA.)

The number of international development assistance agencies is large—so large that many developing countries find that complying with all their separate requirements and expectations can be a serious drain on their limited governmental capacities. The principal assistance agencies can be gathered into four categories:

- *Bilateral agencies.* Most of the 30 OECD countries have foreign aid programs. In addition, in a category all its own, the European Union now maintains one of the largest assistance operations, independent of its members' own programs.

- *UN development agencies.* The UN system's numerous funds, programs, and specialized agencies were discussed in the preceding section.

- *International financial institutions.* Here we have the World Bank and the regional development banks such as the InterAmerican Development Bank and the Asian Development Bank. The role of the World Bank in shaping the environment–development dialogue is large relative to all others.

- *The Global Environment Facility.* The Global Environment Facility (GEF) is extremely important for our purposes since its funding is targeted at the global challenges and support for environmental treaties.

The Global Environment Facility (GEF)

The Global Environment Facility (GEF) was established in 1991 to help developing countries finance efforts to address global environmental challenges. It now works in six areas of global environmental protection: biodiversity, climate change, international waters, ozone depletion, land degradation, and persistent organic pollutants.

Funded by the (richer) donor countries, the GEF has provided $4.5 billion in grants for projects in developing countries. The GEF has also coordinated an addition $14.5 billion in cofinancing from other national and international aid and development agencies. GEF projects are then managed by three implementing agencies. Seven executing agencies contribute and assist in management and administration of GEF projects.

GEF Implementing and Executing Agencies

UN Environment Programme (UNEP)	African Development Bank
UN Development Programme (UNDP)	Asian Development Bank
The World Bank	Inter-American Development Bank
European Bank for Reconstruction & Development	UN Food & Agricultural Organization
International Fund for Agricultural Development	UN Industrial Development Organization

NGOs play a role in the development and monitoring of GEF projects and are guaranteed 10 seats for GEF Council meetings.

Today, most international development assistance agencies have adopted respectably pro-environmental policies and guidelines. The question remains whether their funding for such things as sustainable agriculture, sustainable livelihoods, clean energy, environmental regulation, sanitation and safe water, and forest and biodiversity protection will grow from modest components of their funding categories and reach levels commensurate with the size of the challenges. This question is particularly pertinent for the World Bank, which is the dominant actor in the international development assistance community.

Development assistance can have three major roles in protecting the global environment: (1) injecting environmental objectives into ongoing economic development plans and projects of all types, (2) promoting environmental programs and projects that help meet global environmental challenges through actions at the local and national levels, and (3) assisting in building the in-country capacity to participate meaningfully in the negotiation and implementation of international accords. Most developing countries are chronically short of the resources and skills needed in each of these areas. Many even have difficulty participating meaningfully in the proliferation of annual treaty-by-treaty negotiations, meetings of governing boards of intergovernmental bodies, and international conferences and summits.

An underlying reality is that countries vary dramatically in their ability to formulate and enforce environmental policies, whether domestic or international. In the 1970s most countries of the world created new national bodies responsible for environmental protection. While industrial countries typically have environmental agencies that enjoy bureaucratic autonomy and sufficient administrative resources to develop and deploy environmental policies (namely, stable budgets, professional staffing, and the means to enforce national laws), these conditions are absent in many developing countries.

Industrial countries are generally induced to comply with international environmental treaty obligations through features in treaties and by the potential of adverse publicity. Treaty designs that stress verification mechanisms may be adequate to induce countries to live up to their obligations, especially when those countries value their international reputations. Information made public through various channels can pressure firms and countries to improve their behavior.

For developing countries, though, the matter is often different. Many of these countries need international assistance to improve administrative and policymaking capabilities, to improve domestic enforcement, to establish the economic and technological wherewithal to improve the quality of their environments, and to encourage the roles of civil society NGOs. In these areas, international development assistance can be essential.

If development assistance agencies are strongly promoting sensible environmental policies in their policy dialogues and projects in developing countries, and if the developing world perceives the industrial countries as being genuinely helpful to their interests on both environment and economic fronts, willing to foot a fair share of the bill, and setting a positive example, then these circumstances will have a strongly positive effect on developing country commitment to sustainability and environmental protection.

The World Trade Organization, Environment, Trade, and Globalization

Environmental protection has proceeded since the late 1980s within a broader international political context of international trade liberalization and other aspects of economic globalization. Nations have been trying to promote efficient commerce among their economies in order to promote economic growth. Many observers continue to wonder if environmental protection and globalization are at odds with one another or whether they are reconcilable or even mutually supportive.

Three positions dominate the debate over trade, the environment, and globalization. Free trade environmentalists emphasize the economic and environmental benefits of trade liberalization, arguing that the elimination of trade barriers accelerates economic growth and thus generates more resources that can be devoted to environmental protection and other social projects. Some authors have argued that countries' environmental performance improves above gross national product (GNP) per capita levels of around $6,000. Thus, their primary policy impulse is to maximize economic growth and hope that resources get applied to environmental protection and that the newer industries and factories stimulated by economic growth adopt clean technologies in their operations.

Fierce critics of globalization contend that globalization undermines local communities and livelihoods, increasing inequality in the process, and that the growth it typically succeeds in promoting is unregulated growth occurring at the expense of the environment. They argue that globalization divests national and local authorities of control over their own destinies, and they fear that growth will rely on highly polluting activities that are no longer attractive to industrialized societies.

The pragmatic moderates are in the middle. Unlike the antiglobalization critics, they see a continued role for trade liberalization and globalization. Unlike free trade environmentalists, they are skeptical that increasing economic activity automatically results in a better environment. They see the growth spurred by globalization contributing to environmental progress in a way that is partial, highly selective, and late. Consequently, pragmatic moderates look to the institutional mechanisms available internationally to mitigate the potential for environmental destruction from expanded trade and globalization.

Many of the debates about trade, globalization, and the environment have focused on the activities of the WTO and the North American Free Trade Association (NAFTA), both of which have been led by the larger industrial nations. A particular issue that has received much attention is whether certain environmental protection efforts violate international trade agreements. For example, can a country ban the sale of a product not produced in an environmentally friendly way and, in the process, ban the import of such a product? Disputes have persisted since 1991, when the WTO's precursor, the General Agreement on Tariffs and Trade (GATT), declared illegal the U.S.'s unilateral ban on imported Mexican tuna caught in a manner that the United States claimed endangered dolphins. The dolphin-safe label on cans of tuna sold in the United States is the labeling mechanism by which that U.S. effort was enforced. Subsequently, there have been a number of decisions taken in the WTO's dispute settlement process that may have opened a way to reconcile tensions between trade expansion and environmental protection. The GATT provides that governments cannot discriminate between domestic and imported goods on the basis of the process by which a product was made, if they are "like goods." By interpreting "like goods" in an environmentally friendly way, by broad application of GATT's

> Many of the debates about trade, globalization, and the environment have focused on the activities of the **WTO** and the North American Free Trade Association (NAFTA), both of which have been led by the larger industrial nations.

exemption for "necessary" environmental protection measures, and by development of universal standards that endorse product quality, ways may be found to minimize future trade–environment conflicts.

Daniel Esty and others have argued for greater environmental sensitivity to be folded into the world trading system. In *Greening the GATT,* Esty points to ways that the substantive rules of the GATT could be adjusted to better reflect pollution control and natural resource management efforts. He believes the procedures of the WTO can be made more transparent and open to nontrade experts, giving the WTO greater legitimacy as it addresses "trade and environment" disputes, and that efforts to promote trade liberalization and environmental protection can be made mutually reinforcing if both the trade community and the environmental policy world realign their rules and institutions to reflect the concerns of those on the other side of the "trade–environment divide."[1]

The WTO has tried to respond to some of its critics. The procedures for appealing alleged environmental barriers to trade have been made more transparent. The members of the arbitration panels are now publicly announced, and their work and findings are promptly made accessible on the WTO's website. The individuals responsible for making determinations on trade and environment disputes remain within the trade law community and thus are generally not sensitive to arguments about the need for preserving environmental standards. For this reason and others, environmentalists continue to critique the WTO reforms. WTO defenders argue that the findings of recent WTO tribunals are more nuanced and that a new body of pragmatic trade law is appearing.

The North American Free Trade zone, established in 1994, seeks to eliminate barriers to trade between the United States, Canada, and Mexico. (National rights to bourbon, Canadian whiskey, and tequila are specifically protected.) To get the agreement approved by U.S. labor and environmental NGOs, provisions were introduced to protect labor and environmental standards in each country. Thus, if any of the three governments is seen to be not enforcing environmental standards, a group in any of the countries may petition the NAFTA Commission on Environmental Cooperation and allege that environmental laws are not being implemented. This institutional arrangement is almost unprecedented in international relations because it gives NGOs and other nonstate actors the right to formally challenge the legitimacy of governments' actions. In practice, although several dozen petitions have been filed, few of the challenges have produced results. A successful challenge requires a two-thirds vote of the three governments in the region.

Civil Society and Governance Without Governments

The concept of global governance is broad enough to include major initiatives by civil society actors outside of government—private business and NGOs—and in recent years they have increasingly seized available opportunities to participate.

Perhaps best known in this regard are the many private initiatives involving ecolabeling and product certification. Referring to these as non-state market driven (NSMD) governance systems, Benjamin Cashore has noted that they "derive their policymaking authority not from the state, but from the manipulation of global markets and attention to customer preferences."[2] The goal of affecting consumer purchases by awarding a green "seal of approval," or eco-label, to products and services with the least environmental impacts has been applied to forest products, fish products, paper products, new buildings, tourism facilities and operations, and many others. While governments can be involved in these efforts, as the U.S. government is in rating the energy performance of autos and consumer appliances, many schemes have come about through NGO initiatives, often in partnership with the private sector. The product certification work of the Forest Stewardship Council (FSC) and the Marine Stewardship Council are examples of achieving some measure of international governance without governments. Analyses of NSMD certification reveal significant support for the idea of forest certification in North America and Europe but intense debate about which system is the most appropriate. How to build support for private authority in developing countries is another major challenge facing those promoting not just forest certification but the range of other initiatives emerging in tourism, mining, food production, coffee, and other sectors.[3]

> *The goal of affecting consumer purchases by awarding a green "seal of approval," or eco-label, to products and services with the least environmental impacts has been applied to forest products, fish products, paper products, new buildings, tourism facilities and operations, and many others.*

Industry groups have launched a number of self-policing initiatives, including voluntary corporate codes of conduct and standards for environmental management systems. A leading example of the former is the International Chamber of Commerce's Business Charter for Sustainable Development, to which over 2,000 companies worldwide have pledged support. ICC principle number one requires companies to recognize environmental management as among the highest corporate priorities. The International Organization for Standardization has launched an ISO 14000 series, which provides voluntary standards for environmental audits, performance evaluations, product life cycle assessments, and product labeling. Several thousand companies internationally have been certified in compliance with ISO 14000.

More focused and deeper changes in corporate conduct have stemmed from the commitments that scores of major companies have made to reduce their climate-changing greenhouse gas emissions. DuPont, Shell, Alcoa, British Petroleum, and many others have volunteered commitments to reduce their greenhouse gas emissions to at least 15 percent below their 1990 levels by 2010. A significant number of major corporations are now cooperating in a greenhouse gas reduction program organized by the private Chicago Climate Exchange.

NGOs have had success with both advocacy campaigns and on-the-ground conservation initiatives. The Natural Resources Defense Council's Biogems campaign, for example, has brought international pressure to bear on the Mitsubishi Corporation, forcing it to withdraw plans for a salt facility that would have harmed a whale calving area in Mexico, and on timber companies in British Columbia, halting plans to clear-cut on 3.5 million acres of forest until an ecologically sensitive management plan is developed. NGOs are today working to save threatened landscapes on an unprecedented scale. Major conservation groups such as the World Wildlife Fund, Conservation International, and The Nature Conservancy, allied with many local groups and host governments, are leading efforts to protect large areas of the Amazon, a Yucatan to Yukon corridor through the Western mountain ranges, and a series of 34 biodiversity hot spots around the globe.

One area of private governance likely to have a major long-term impact is the emergence of a rapidly growing green investor community. Spearheaded by the Coalition for Environmentally Responsible Economies (CERES) and other groups, many pension funds, socially and environmentally screened mutual funds, and other investors large and small are focusing their investments and their shareholder votes in ways that encourage a higher level of corporate environmental performance. Over $3 trillion in investment assets have now come together in the Investor Network on Climate Risk organized by CERES to press for reductions in greenhouse gas emissions.

Though it is unlikely in the extreme that voluntary, "bottom up" initiatives in civil society can supplant the need for concerted governmental and intergovernmental action, they can both contribute significantly and pave the way—demonstrating concern, providing solutions, and making governmental action more likely. For this reason and others, environmental NGOs have been enormously important in international environmental affairs in the recent past.

In sum, civil society organizations help to compensate for many of the flaws in governmental stewardship. They help to mobilize domestic and transnational actors around key issues, and they encourage agenda setting and compliance. They can establish informal but effective goals and norms. Yet they are but one of many classes of actors necessary for the success of global environmental governance.

VI

Paths to the Future: A Second Attempt at Global Environmental Governance?

WE HAVE SEEN THAT OVER THE PAST FEW DECADES HUGE INTERNATIONAL efforts have been expended in an effort to cope with the major threats to the global environment. In many respects this exercise of planetary stewardship has been impressive. But the underlying reality is that these efforts have been inadequate, and the disturbing trends that drove action in the first place by and large continue. The question then is how best to improve global environmental governance. Here there are many opinions. In this final chapter we examine some of the recommendations that have been offered.

To begin this inquiry, it is useful to start with a broad framework. Were cultural anthropologists to look at our environmental politics, they might identify four overarching worldviews regarding nature and human societies. Worldviews powerfully organize our thinking by presenting a tacit set of cause and effect relations that we apply when considering an issue, and also by providing a screen to select out factors that are not germane to the question at hand. Think of them as an interrelated set of biases that affect how we see the world.

One worldview is that of the cornucopians, who might also be called market liberals, where we use *liberal* in the European sense.[1] They tend to see nature as boundless and thus unlikely to exercise significant constraints over human action. They are optimistic about the economy's ability to innovate and develop ever more efficient and cleaner technologies, thus keeping environmental problems under control. Economic growth, in their view, facilitates technological innovation and solutions to natural resource scarcity.

Malthusians, on the other hand, see nature and resources as finite and exercising constraints on human action. The natural environment has a "carrying capacity" limiting the scale of economic activity, especially the scale of resource consumption and pollution. Ecosystems and the services they provide are in danger of being lost due to harvesting above regeneration rates or pollution beyond assimilative capacities. Modern-day Malthusians, neo-Malthusians, drawing on the latest science, might better be called bioenvironmentalists.

Reformists or institutionalists see nature as resilient within some range of parameters that are themselves dynamic. They appreciate the Malthusian dilemma, but they emphasize that skillful policy guidance relying on close connections among governments, scientists, and nongovernmental organizations (NGOs) and indigenous communities is capable of recognizing emerging scarcities and threats and devising responses that are appropriate to resolve them. Strong and effective institutions at the national and international levels can make this possible. This perspective calls for deliberative procedural responses to environmental risks—procedures stressing the need for involving multiple voices in formulating and assessing policy responses. Appropriately guided, economic growth and development are seen as consistent with environmental preservation.

Social greens dispute the utility of discussing resource availability in the abstract; they argue that the true questions have to do with power within society and with inequitable resource access and distribution. They look at the social context in which resource decisions are taken and focus on participatory and redistributive policies to address questions of resource scarcity. They question the political impartiality of "expertise" and the ability of governments as commonly constituted to guide sensible behavior.

Throughout the period from Stockholm to Johannesburg, and still today, cornucopian market liberals have very much controlled the actual levers of power and decision making. As necessary, they have made concessions to institutional reformists, and the structures we reviewed in chapters 4 and 5 have been the result. These patterns continue to be the dominant ones in international environmental affairs today.

Meanwhile, in more academic and wonkish circles, other debates have proceeded. Much of the environmental discourse in the 1970s and 1980s could be described as Malthusians vs. cornucopians, both rather crudely conceived. The debate set off by the original 1972 *Limits to Growth* report is a good example of this.

More recently, many scholars and writers have started to look more deeply at prospects for coping effectively with global environmental challenges. In this community, one can identify two camps—the institutional reformists who want to make the system of treaty regimes and international institutions work much better, and the bioenvironmentalists and social greens who believe much deeper changes are necessary.

Reformists tend to believe that our first attempt at global environmental governance with its focus on international environmental law is basically on the right track, that international environmental law is a young field now rapidly developing and holding much promise as evidenced by some notable successes, and that much "social learning" is occurring through the international processes that have been launched, so that a period of rapid, much-needed progress is now becoming possible, particularly if reforms can be implemented to strengthen the way international environmental law is done.

The bioenvironmentalists, while agreeing on the need to strengthen the current approach, are more skeptical. They would argue that the current focus on regimes is too one-dimensional, that there are inherent difficulties with international law and lawmaking that make it unrealistic to expect regimes to accomplish what is needed, and that deeper and more difficult changes will be needed in order to move to environmental sustainability.

Reformists tend to believe in the ability of societies to design collective governance arrangements that can contribute to a more sustainable future. Bioenvironmentalists are far more skeptical about the ability of societies to respond to environmental threats through reliance on diplomacy and traditional policymaking.

Reformists say we are doing better than we have in the past. Bioenvironmentalists say that such efforts aren't good enough. Reformists point to instrumental processes that contribute to improvements. They see selective advances in environmental regimes and argue that political reform can greatly improve the process. Bioenvironmentalists argue that problems are too urgent and broad for incremental approaches.

In this chapter we explore these two perspectives.

Reformist Visions: How to Make the System Work Better

Much of the academic research on international environmental affairs in recent years has focused on environmental regimes and related institutions and processes. Out of this research has emerged a long list of reforms needed to improve and strengthen the current system. The scope and importance of the changes needed are testimony to the seriousness of the deficiencies in the existing system.

As we saw in chapter 4, "effectiveness" has been widely studied, as academics and policymakers have sought to identify factors that contributed to better international environmental cooperation and protection. Effective international arrangements are those that lead nations to make policy changes that further the goals of the arrangements, with the result that there are improvements in environmental quality. If we know what conditions and initiatives further the effectiveness and success of international regimes, then we will know where to invest for better results.

Examples of effective regimes, where the environment is confidently believed to be improved or on the path to improvement, include the stratospheric ozone regime; the European acid rain treaty; efforts to protect the North Sea, the Baltic Sea, and Antarctic living resources; the regulation of ocean dumping and marine pollution from ships; and, less clearly, the control of the endangered species trade. Results are much more disappointing for desertification, deforestation, marine protection, management of toxic substances, and nitrogen pollution. Climate change and biodiversity have seen some changes in national policies, but these changes are inadequate to address the underlying problems.

Many of the factors leading to more effective regimes can be grouped under three headings: building the environment for cooperation, building national capacity, and building national concern. Let's discuss each of the three C's—cooperative environment, capacity, and concern.[2]

Cooperative Environment

A number of factors can improve the context within which environmental negotiations are conducted and thus make it easier for states to reach meaningful agreements. For starters, the number of participants is important. A relatively *small number* of actors—whether private business corporations or nations at the negotiating table—makes it easier to identify culprits and to develop meaningful policies to mitigate the problems. The involvement of business stakeholders in negotiations can make the arrangements more effective in the end, but that is only feasible if small numbers are involved. A relatively small number of nations engaged in making decisions facilitates reaching agreement; achieving consensus with large numbers can be very difficult. Governments have grown accustomed to relying on caucuses and blocs of countries to reduce the difficulties created by large numbers of countries in the United Nations. *Continuing negotiations* rather than one-shot negotiating sessions are better at generating meaningful compromises. Over time states grow more familiar with one another's positions and are also willing to make concessions at one meeting in the anticipation that those concessions may be reciprocated at future meetings. A high profile for negotiations also encourages breakthroughs and meaningful commitments that midlevel bureaucrats lack the authority to make. Thus, some COPs and other meetings now include high-level ministerial sessions before or after the longer negotiations, at which such deals may be presented.

Voting rules are extremely important. Reaching consensus makes it difficult to achieve agreements with real bite—any government important to the outcome that wants to throw a wrench into the works can do so—yet consensus decision making is the norm in treaty negotiations since sovereignty requires that no nation be bound against its will. One way around these difficulties is for governments to agree to waive consensus-based decision making in certain situations. Progress has been made in this regard, and more is needed. As has happened with the Montreal Protocol and the Stockholm Convention on Persistent Organic Pollutants, the COP can be empowered to make certain types of regulatory decisions that would not need to be ratified as separate treaties, and procedures can be introduced whereby a two-thirds supermajority, a double majority (a majority of both industrial and developing countries), or even a mere majority of the COP members could make decisions binding for all. Conceivably a COP could even delegate certain rulemaking or standard-setting powers to an expert body. The COP would limit itself to providing the broad policy framework and providing a check against abuse of discretion, much as Congress and the federal courts supervise decision making in U.S. regulatory agencies.

Well-designed treaties incorporate explicit provisions that encourage meaningful cooperation and compliance by parties. Three factors have been identified as critical: formal enforcement provisions, verification measures, and environmental monitoring. Each of these is likely to improve compliance, as well as indirectly contributing to more ambitious regimes because nations are more confident that requirements will be widely respected and enforced. *Formal enforcement provisions* include economic sanctions against parties that are in violation and legal provisions for arbitration over disputes in interpretation or for enforcing sanctions. Curiously, few international environmental treaties contain strong sanctions or compliance mechanisms. While most treaties include legal language for arbitration, arbitration proceedings are rarely initiated. To the extent that environmental treaties are effective, it is through nations' own calculations of their self-interest, rather than through fears of consequences of noncompliance.

Verification is important to assure that parties are living up to their obligations. Most regimes include verification measures that collect information about parties' compliance. Nations are more likely to comply with their international obligations if infractions are promptly and accurately reported. Treaties vary widely in terms of who collects this information and how frequently. Since self-reporting can run the risk of nations misrepresenting their records, impartial third parties can sometimes be used. For instance, after the Cold War ended it was discovered that the Soviets had been routinely lying about their whale catches and the amount of radioactive wastes they were dumping in the ocean. In practice most treaties rely on a complicated mix of verification arrangements.

Environmental monitoring is also important for providing an accurate picture of conditions and trends in the environment. Robust monitoring programs encourage stronger treaties, because nations can ascertain if their efforts are having an impact, and can develop new policies if new threats are identified or if earlier concerns are shown to be exaggerated.

Two characteristics of the international organizations within which negotiations are being conducted can influence outcomes and countries' willingness to cooperate. *Horizontal linkages* refer to overlapping memberships in organizations or regimes in which countries are members. Nations may make compromises in one set of negotiations when they know that they will be closely involved with the same states in other venues. Nations that often interact with one another across a variety of environmental and other issues are also more likely to comply with obligations, out of a need to maintain a broader reputation for being good international citizens. For instance, in the 1980s the United Kingdom suffered from its reputation as being the "dirty man of Europe." Seeking to shed this reputation led the United Kingdom to support a stronger acid rain regime than it had initially desired. The European Union is dense with horizontal linkages, so members are more likely to comply with EU directives. Similarly, EU members are more likely to comply with environmental treaties when those treaties become part of EU commitments. *Vertical linkages* refer to broadly accepted international norms that can be applied to govern behavior in particular domains. Thus, if environmental issues are negotiated within the World Trade Organization (WTO), they will be subject to broader norms of promoting free trade and minimizing barriers to trade. If they are conducted under United Nations Environment Programme (UNEP) auspices, then norms of environmental protection and sustainable development will be accorded higher priority.

Capacity

With any new law requiring serious efforts at implementation, new capacities must be built in and out of government. Capacity constraints are especially severe in most of the developing countries. There are various forms of capacity-increasing transfers that can be used to reward countries and support implementation and compliance: *financial transfers, technology transfers,* and *knowledge transfers.* Each can have a role in inducing countries to support and comply with environmental treaties. Financial transfers provide money for improving compliance with international obligations and are particularly attractive to poorer developing countries. Technology transfers include sales and gifts of environmental technology and technical equipment for environmental monitoring. Knowledge transfers consist of training programs for government officials in environmental management, monitoring, and verification activities. Knowledge transfers also include environmental training programs for national scientists and even NGOs.

Concern

Heightened national concern can pressure governments to take stronger action on the environment. One key variable accounting for policy change is the degree of domestic environmental pressure. Effective regimes and organizations have included programs for building public concern, such as public education campaigns that include TV, radio, and other media presentations. Public concern is also built when participation of national NGOs and scientists is enhanced. Building environmental norms at the international level can heighten national concern, as can publicizing monitoring results.

The following table summarizes some of the lessons learned about improving the effectiveness of the environmental treaty process.

Improving the Effectiveness of Environmental Governance

	Factors	Effects
Cooperative environment	Numbers (small number of actors whose behavior needs changing, relatively small number of actors involved in developed policy responses)	Increase likelihood of achieving compromise on an environmental regime.
	Voting rules	
	Frequency of negotiations	
	Perceived fairness	
	High profile	
	Formal enforcement provisions (sanctions,arbitration procedures)	
	Verification	
	Monitoring	
	Horizontal linkages	
	Vertical linkages	
Capacity building	Financial transfers	Improve ability to comply with obligations, and also increase the likelihood of a stronger negotiated regime because governments will be confident that others will reciprocate their actions.
	Technology transfers	
	Knowledge transfers	
Building national concern	Public education	Increase democratic states' willingness to participate in negotiated regimes, and possibly educate elites and state officials about new state interests.
	Norm building	
	Mobilizing scientific networks	
	Providing accurate environmental data through monitoring	

Viewing the question in a somewhat different way, we can also consider some of the conditions one would want to promote within individual countries in order to promote the success of the treaty process:

- Peace and stability
- Favorable economic conditions and the absence of financial or other economic crises
- An open, democratic society and an independent, effective media presence
- A high level of public concern and active NGOs

- The presence of rule of law and a culture of compliance with international law

- The human and institutional capacities in government to participate meaningfully at all stages

One Summary of Factors Linked to Successful International Environmental Law

"However defined, the list of factors linked to effectiveness is almost embarrassingly long. Credible analysts do offer the following more manageable list. A fair amount of scientific consensus about the existence and cause of the international problem is fundamental, as is political support within the participating nations. The organizational capabilities of the secretariat and other implementing institutions should be supported. The secretariat needs to have resources and information. The regime institutions must be able to create ad hoc alliances among themselves, and the regime must have an understandable and legitimate dispute resolution process. It should be open to public and scientific input. NGO involvement of a clearly determined type is important. A modest entry commitment should suffice for nation-state participation. A compliance-promoting mechanism, whether a taxing capacity or a subsidy or trust fund, and recognition of varying capacities of developed and developing nations are essential.

"The regime should be based on consensual understandings of clear policy objectives. It should ensure to all stakeholders, including NGOs and the public, open communication and access to relevant information. It should establish and strengthen norms for cooperation, implementation, and compliance. These should be promulgated by a legitimate, competent, recognized authority with a willingness and ability to interpret treaty terms and to enforce them. Questions of liability and sanctions should be answered clearly. The institutions involved should foster collaboration and cooperation in agenda setting, negotiating, and bargaining. Public participation should be encouraged not only during policy formation but also in implementation. The treaty regime should embody consensus-building mechanisms and provide for an ongoing forum to manage issues. Finally, the regime's organizations must have sufficient human and financial resources."

DiMento, J. F. C. 2003. *The Global Environment and International Law*. Austin: University of Texas Press, 139–40.

Viewed this way, we can see that the potential success of international environmental law can be easily undermined by the unfortunate tendency to neglect the social and political context in which international agreements are arrived at and then implemented. Human societies will never achieve perfection, but they are going to have to try a lot harder at it if international environmental law is to succeed.

Reformist Visions: Major Innovations

Beyond these ideas, there are three other reformist visions that deserve special attention. The first two involve creating a World Environment Organization and opening the door for the public to participate in the treaty process much as it does in the domestic legislative and enforcement processes. The third involves using what have come to be called "global issue networks."

A World Environment Organization

It is strange, some say, to have a WHO and a WTO and not have a WEO. If one were writing on a clean slate—approaching afresh the question of what international regulatory organizations should be created—the case for a World Environment Organization would be among the very strongest. Many of the arguments brought forth for "federalizing" U.S. and European environmental policy also support the need for globalizing environmental

---

SOUNDINGS • **Reuters News Service**

EU TAKES ACTION AGAINST TWELVE STATES OVER ENVIRONMENT

BRUSSELS, JULY 12, 2005—The European Commission took legal action against 12 EU states on Monday for failing to carry out proper environmental impact assessments of land use, road construction and waste management schemes.

Austria, Belgium, Cyprus, Greece, Spain, Finland, Italy, Luxembourg, Malta, Netherlands, Portugal and Slovakia are the states concerned.

Failure to comply with European Union rules could land those countries in the EU's top court, which can impose fines on them.

The 12 states have failed to properly implement an EU law ensuring that proper environmental impact assessments are carried out before new roads are built or waste management schemes approved, the EU executive said in a statement.

protection: we live in a world where pollution knows no boundaries and where trade, technology, and investment flows are increasingly international. A WEO could be quite modest or quite powerful. In one model, UNEP would become a specialized agency of the United Nations and would thus gain in stature, size, and independence. This metamorphosis would enlarge its financial resources and provide a more efficient and effective structure for governance and leadership. The next step in increasing the role of the new WEO would bring the various environmental treaties together under it. The most ambitious idea would create a world environment agency entrusted with setting international standards and enforcing them against laggard countries.

To build a WEO, it might be wise to begin at the modest end of the spectrum and gradually strengthen the new organization as trust and confidence increase. Initially, a new UN specialized agency for the environment could incorporate UNEP, reflect modern organizational concepts, and do the following:

- Provide an international vehicle for national environmental ministers, much as WHO is the focal point for health ministries around the world

- Promote international environmental law, including new treaties, and provide a common secretariat and dispute resolution services for the various existing treaty regimes

- Serve as a global environmental watchdog, ombudsman, and catalyst

- Provide global monitoring of conditions and trends, as well as foresight and early warning

- Develop consensus around informal international goals and mobilize financing and launch campaigns related to them

- Assess and report on national and international performance and progress

- Coordinate and sponsor relevant scientific research

This WEO would also provide an international center of expertise on what works and what does not in environmental law, policy, and management. Countries building environmental programs at national and regional levels could seek advice and assistance. Information and data banks could be accessed by all. Thanks to an outpouring of scholarship, we now know much better the criteria for success in international environmental regimes. Future efforts in global environmental governance will have to build on this knowledge, pursue science-based and data-driven approaches to "smart regulation," and use market-based mechanisms such as emissions trading, which has been successfully deployed against acid rain and is now being used to protect climate. More focused agreements involving smaller numbers of parties should be one avenue of pursuit; another should be agreements that address explicitly the need for technology transformation.

Opening the System to the Public

Reforming the current treaty system also involves providing the public with greater access to the process, including access to the information needed for responsible participation. Until citizens can have their say in international fora, get the information they need, submit petitions for action and complaints for noncompliance, participate in hearings and initiate judicial proceedings to enforce international law—all the things that are available in many countries at the national level—international environmental law and policy will never have the dynamism it so badly needs.

Global Issue Networks

Our final reformist vision is to take a major step outside the world of conventional regimes and explore the idea of global issue networks. The goal here, like that of conventional regimes, is to reach an effective "global accord" on major environmental issues, but the path to that goal is quite different.

Our story begins with the realization that, while the intergovernmental system is often bogged down in endless and ineffectual wordsmithing, enormous new potential exists in the world outside governments. In *The Coming Democracy: New Rules for Running a New World*, Ann Florini describes this emergence: "New systems of global decision making are emerging that go beyond cooperation between states to a much messier agglomeration of ad hoc mechanisms for solving the many and varied transnational problems. No one is planning this system. It is evolving, with many disparate actors who are largely unaware of the roles of other sectors and their relationships to other issues. The private sector and the amorphous third sector of nongovernmental organizations that are grouped under the heading of "civil society" are becoming key figures in transnational governance, filling some of the gaps that governments are leaving open. Increasingly . . . agreements are being worked out and implemented directly between the private sector and activist groups on issues ranging from environmental protection to labor standards."[3]

The most elaborate discussion of the why and how of global issue networks is that provided by J. F. Rischard in *High Noon: 20 Global Problems, 20 Years to Solve Them*. Rischard sees a global issue network, say one on deforestation in the tropics, beginning with a "constitutional phase" in which some existing agency hosts a convening event to which stakeholders from governments, NGOs North and South, and potentially affected business and commercial interests are invited. The work then moves to the "norm-producing phase" in which a rough consensus is arrived on key questions: What exactly is the problem? Where do we want to be in 20 years? How do we get there? What should the norms and standards be? In the "implementation phase," major emphasis is on "creating reputation effects through naming-and-shaming." Countries and other players are rated against the norms, and public and peer pressure is deployed to promote better performance from laggards.[4]

These emerging processes would not be possible without the growing vitality and, thanks to the Internet, the growing connectivity of the international NGO community. In *Environmental Activism and World Civic Politics*, Paul Wapner reiterates Florini's points and stresses the growing roles of this community: "Over the past few decades . . . a host of citizen-organized activist groups have arisen—or greatly expanded their size and scope—with the aim of protecting the earth. While data are sketchy, it is estimated that presently there are over 100,000 nongovernmental organizations (NGOs) working, in some capacity, for environmental protection, and a majority of these are activist groups. Perhaps more impressive than numbers, the scope and power of environmental activist organizations has dramatically increased. In recent years, a number of groups have become transnational. They are organized across state boundaries and work toward environmental protection at the global level. The budgets of the largest of these groups are greater than the amounts most countries spend on environmental issues and at least double what the United Nations Environment Programme (UNEP) spends annually for its work. . . .

"To be sure, nation-states are essential in addressing environmental issues and activist efforts to pressure them are significant in world environmental affairs. Additionally, however, there are other arenas for organizing and carrying out efforts that are separate from the realm of government. These other arenas can be found in what has been called global civil society, and the attempt to use them for environmental protection purposes is a form of world civic politics. Transnational environmental groups practice world civic politics in addition to lobbying, and their work along these lines has become an important component of environmental politics more generally."[5]

Of course, as Wapner notes, the state system is not withering away, and governments remain enormously important. Therefore, analysis provided by Anne-Marie Slaughter, dean of Princeton's Woodrow Wilson School, is pertinent. In *A New World Order* she stresses that it is essential to involve governmental officials in these global issue networks. They are the actors "who can be held to account through a variety of political mechanisms." She continues: "Understood as a form of global governance, government networks meet these needs. As commercial and civic organizations have already discovered, their networked form is ideal for providing the speed and flexibility necessary to function effectively in an information age. But unlike amorphous 'global policy networks' . . . in which it is never clear who is exercising power on behalf of whom, these are networks composed of national government officials, either appointed by elected officials or directly elected themselves. Best of all, they can perform many of the functions of a world government—legislation, administration, and adjudication—without the form."[6]

Global and regional networking is proving its importance daily. As Slaughter points out, "Terrorists, arms dealers, money launderers, drug dealers, traffickers in women and children, and the modern pirates of intellectual property all operate through global networks. So, increasingly, do governments." What all these authorities are saying is that it is time to apply a more organized type of stakeholder networking to the serious business of reversing global environmental deterioration.

Alternative Visions: How to Change the System

Many observers, including our neo-Malthusian bioenvironmentalists and the Social Greens, argue that in order seriously to address global environmental threats, deeper changes must be undertaken that address the underlying causes of such problems, though they do not all agree on what the root causes are. Some tend to see the causes of international environmental decline as deriving from structural factors having to do with economic inequality, an absence of political representation, and undeveloped environmental sensibilities among the majority of the world's population.

Some of those urging these alternative approaches see them as important complements to environmental regimes; others see little hope for the regime approach and are disparaging regarding its prospects. In this section we review several of the alternatives that stress the need for progress in areas other than regimes and other international agreements.

Addressing the Underlying Drivers: Beyond Dealing with Symptoms

Three books by longtime observers of the global environmental scene appeared in 2003–2004, each reaching similar conclusions on a number of key issues. Lester Brown's *Plan B: Rescuing a Planet under Stress and a Civilization in Trouble,* Paul and Anne Ehrlich's *One with Nineveh: Politics, Consumption and the Human Future,* and Gus Speth's *Red Sky at Morning:America and the Crisis of the Global Environment* each contend that (1) global environmental conditions are steadily worsening, (2) current efforts to address them are inadequate, and (3) major new initiatives are needed, and these initiatives should address the underlying drivers of deterioration—the root causes. These works share many common elements regarding the identification of these drivers and what should be done about them, including similar views on four of the drivers: population and poverty, technology, consumption, and the current market system.

Here is Brown's *Plan B* on the imperative of action on population:"Early in this new century, the world is facing many long-standing social challenges, including hunger, illiteracy, and disease. If developing countries add nearly 3 billion people by mid-century, as projected, population growth will continue to undermine efforts to improve the human condition . . .

"As a species, our failure to control our numbers is taking a frightening toll. Slowing population growth is the key to eradicating poverty and its distressing symptoms, and conversely, eradicating poverty is the key to slowing population growth. With time running out, the urgency of moving simultaneously on both fronts seems clear.

"The challenge is to create quickly the social conditions that will accelerate the shift to smaller families. Among these conditions are universal education, good nutrition, and prevention of infectious diseases. We now have the knowledge and the resources to reach these goals. In an increasingly integrated world, we also have a vested interest in doing so."[7]

And Speth's *Red Sky at Morning* on the need for a new technology: "We urgently need a worldwide environmental revolution in technology—a rapid ecological modernization of industry and agriculture. The prescription is straightforward but challenging: the principal way to reduce pollution and resource consumption while achieving expected economic growth is to bring about a wholesale transformation in the technologies that today dominate manufacturing, energy, transportation, and agriculture. . . . The focus should be on 'dematerializing' the economy through a new generation of environmentally benign technologies that sharply reduce the consumption of natural resources and the generation of residual products per unit of economic output. The good news here is that across a wide front, technologies that would bring about a vast improvement are either available or soon can be."[8]

Speth goes on to provide an extensive list of newer technologies in renewable energy, precision energy use, hydrogen, fuel cells, automotive and light rail design, and so on.

And the Ehrlichs' plea for an end to rampant consumerism in *One With Nineveh*: "In the aggregate, there is abundant evidence that, once basic biological needs for food, shelter, clothing, and health care are met and a standard of living providing some leisure time and recreation is adopted, further consumption doesn't provide much increased satisfaction. The data for this are relatively unambiguous. In the United States, per capita real income (a surrogate for consumption) doubled between 1957 and 1992, but public opinion polls showed no increase in reported happiness. . . .

"There have been minor rebellions against rampant consumerism, as in the voluntary simplicity movement and phenomena such as green labeling (certification of an environmentally benign origin of products). And, perhaps most important, the negative environmental and social consequences related to unfettered American consumerism—suburban sprawl; deteriorating roads, bridges, and schools; degradation of national parks and forests; the growing gap between rich and poor—are increasingly being noticed."[9]

Speth's *Red Sky at Morning* stresses the need to make prices and market signals work for the environment: "We seek a market transition to a world in which market forces are harnessed to environmental ends, particularly by making prices reflect the full environmental costs. . . . Full-cost pricing is everywhere thwarted today by the failure of governments to eliminate environmentally perverse subsidies and to ensure that external environmental costs—including damages to public health, natural resources, and ecosystem services—are captured in market prices. The corrective most needed now is environmentally honest prices.

"Environmental economists make a powerful case for full-cost pricing and have identified a variety of economic instruments that are available to move in this direction. They advocate securing property rights to overcome the 'tragedy of the commons' problem, tradable emission permits, pollution taxes, user fees, shifting subsidies from environmentally damaging activities to beneficial ones, and making polluters and others financially liable for the damages they cause."[10]

The first step in taking action to curb the drivers of deterioration is for governments, NGOs, and business to decide that they must be addressed systematically. From that platform, finding the specific steps the international community can take, together or in loose concert, to reverse these drivers becomes possible. The ongoing efforts to achieve the United Nations Millennium Development Goals may be the best place to focus additional efforts on population and poverty. A good example of how the international community can come together to promote technology transformation is the German-led effort to promote international goals and cooperation for widespread use of wind and other renewable energy technologies. The shift to sustainable patterns of consumption would be furthered by an international agreement on ecolabeling and "product biographies." Interestingly, a recent effort to "get the prices right" came from an unusual source when the WTO moved against U.S., European, and Japanese agricultural subsidies. A serious effort to reduce greenhouse gas emissions, such as that contemplated in the second phase of the Kyoto Protocol process, would also help move toward full-cost, environmentally honest pricing of energy.

Natural Capitalism: Beyond Blinkered Capitalism

In *Natural Capitalism,* Paul Hawken and Amory and Hunter Lovins do not reject capitalism; they merely seek to co-opt and green it. At one level, their prescriptions fit within the previous category of addressing the root causes of global environmental problems: they describe with extraordinary command the way new technology and technique can be put to good use by companies and governments. Similarly, they are clear that governments must intervene to make the market work for the environment rather than against it: "[N]atural capitalism does not aim to discard market economics, nor reject its valid and important principles or its powerful mechanisms. It does suggest that we should vigorously employ markets for their proper purpose as a tool for solving the problems we face, while better understanding markets' boundaries and limitations.

"Many of the excesses of markets can be compensated for by steering their immense forces in more creative and constructive directions. What is required is diligence to understand when and where markets are dysfunctional or misapplied, and to choose the correct targeted actions to help them to operate better while retaining their vigor and vitality.

"For all their power and vitality, markets are only tools. They make a good servant but a bad master and a worse religion. They can be used to accomplish many important tasks, but they can't do everything, and it's a dangerous delusion to begin to believe that they can—especially when they threaten to replace ethics or politics."[11]

But *Natural Capitalism* also offers a radically new vision of how capitalism should work, backed by the hope that the business community, freed from the shackles of the past and empowered by this new vision, will become the principal vehicle for addressing many global environmental challenges. Hawken and the Lovinses see four central strategies toward natural capitalism:

- Radically increased resource productivity in order to slow resource depletion at one end of the value chain and to lower pollution at the other end.

- Redesigned industrial systems that mimic biological ones so that even the concept of wastes is progressively eliminated.

- An economy based on the provision of services rather than the purchase of goods.

- Reversal of worldwide resource deterioration and declines in ecosystem services through major new investments in regenerating natural capital.

Natural Capitalism envisions an extraordinary and hitherto largely unrealized role for business. "The success of resources productivity as a societal strategy may augur an entirely new relationship between business and government. . . . [Business] may need to take positions diametrically opposed to its prior stands and even argue for stricter regulation. . . . It will not be trivial to establish sensible policies. Emphasizing resource productivity will require reversal of two hundred years of policies in taxes, labor, industry and trade, meant to encourage extraction, depletion and disposal. . . . In a few decades, historians may write a history of our times that goes something like this: Now that the private sector has taken its proper place as the main implementer of sustainable practices, simply because they work better and cost less, the 1970s and 1980s approach of micromanagement by intensive government regulation is only a bad memory."[12]

Ecological Economics: Beyond Neoclassical Economics

In their 2004 textbook *Ecological Economics,* Herman Daly and Joshua Farley challenge customary thinking about the economy and economic growth: "More contentious (and more important) is the call by ecological economics for an end to growth. We define growth as an increase in throughput, which is the flow of natural resources from the environment, through the economy, and back to the environment as waste. It is a quantitative increase in the physical dimensions of the economy and/or of the waste stream produced by the economy. This kind of growth, of course, cannot continue indefinitely, as the Earth and its resources are not infinite. While growth must end, this in no way implies an end to development, which we define as qualitative change, realization of potential, evolution toward an improved, but not larger, structure or system—an increase in the quality of goods and services (where quality is measured by the ability to increase human well-being) provided by a given throughput. . . .

"Where conventional economics espouses growth forever, ecological economics envisions a steady-state economy at optimal scale. Each is logical within its own preanalytic vision, and each is absurd from the viewpoint of the other. The difference could not be more basic, more elementary, or more irreconcilable."[13]

Daly and Farley believe we are now in a "full world" where "continued physical expansion of the economy threatens to impose unacceptable costs." They note that the most binding constraint on economic growth may be the waste absorption capacity of the environment rather than resource depletion, long thought to be the likely constraint.

Over the past decade ecological economics has become an increasingly sophisticated analytical system. From the perspective of many of its practitioners, global environmental challenges are unlikely to be met successfully within the framework of neoclassical economics because this well-established system of economic thought recognizes only two of the three key factors—allocation and distribution—but not scale. Theoretically, for any given ecosystem setting, there is an optimum scale of the economy beyond which physical growth in the economy starts costing more than it is worth in terms of human welfare. Practically, Daly and others might maintain we have reached or are past this point. They would see the solution to global environmental challenges in virgin materials taxes and charges on pollution, waste disposal and other environmental damage, and similar measures sufficient to begin to reduce "throughput," the physical size of the economy. Such measures would increase sharply the productivity of natural resources and would be coupled with investments in regenerating the stock of natural capital.

Local Control: Beyond Corporate Globalization

If Hawken and the Lovinses see the possibility of an increasingly positive and constructive role for business, others doubt that global environmental challenges can be addressed unless much is done to curb corporate power and reshape the process of economic globalization now under way.

Much as ecological economics represents a direct challenge to what it sees as the inadequacies in neoclassical economics, the authors of *Alternatives to Economic Globalization: A Better World Is Possible* present a direct challenge to the ascendancy of what they call the "corporate globalists." These authors, brought together by the International Forum on Globalization, are the intellectual leaders of what is often called the antiglobalization movement. Agree with them or disagree, they offer a coherent perspective on what is wrong, why the environment is under such threat, and what should be done about it.

Their assault, they acknowledge, is aimed squarely at the dominant structures of the modern economy and policy: "Since World War II, the driving forces behind economic globalization have been several hundred global corporations and banks that have increasingly woven webs of production, consumption, finance, and culture across borders. Indeed, most of what we eat, drink, wear, drive, and entertain ourselves with today are the products of global corporations.

"These corporations have been aided by global bureaucracies that have emerged over the last half-century, with the overall result being a concentration of economic and political power that is increasingly unaccountable to governments, people, or the planet and that undermines democracy, equity, and environmental sustainability. . . .

"Together these instruments are bringing about the most fundamental redesign of the planet's social, economic, and political arrangements since the Industrial Revolution. They are engineering a power shift of stunning proportions, moving real economic and political power away from national, state, and local governments and communities toward unprecedented centralization of power for global corporations, bankers, and the global bureaucracies they helped create, at the expense of national sovereignty, community control, democracy, diversity, and the natural world. . . .

"The first tenet of the globalization design is to give primary importance to the achievement of ever more rapid, never-ending corporate economic growth—hypergrowth—fueled by the constant search for access to new resources, new and cheaper labor sources, and new markets. . . . To achieve hypergrowth, the emphasis is on the ideological heart of the model—free trade—accompanied by deregulation of corporate activity. The idea is to remove as many impediments as possible to expanded corporate activity."[14]

Environmental deterioration is placed unambiguously at the doorstep of these forces: "Economic globalization is intrinsically harmful to the environment because it is based on ever increasing consumption, exploitation of resources, and waste disposal problems. One of its primary features, export-oriented production, is especially damaging because it is responsible for increasing global transport activity, fossil fuel use, and refrigeration and packaging, while requiring very costly and ecologically damaging new infrastructures such as ports, airports, dams, canals, and so on."[15]

Not much can be done about negative environmental trends, they argue, absent far-reaching changes in the way economic and political power is distributed in modern society. The antiglobalization critique, then, is fundamentally political: "The current and future well-being of humanity depends on transforming the relationships of power within and between societies toward more democratic and mutually accountable modes of managing human affairs that are self-organizing, power-sharing, and minimize the need for coercive central authority."[16]

In response they offer a different vision: "The corporate globalists who meet in posh gatherings to chart the course of corporate globalization in the name of private profits, and the citizen movements that organize to thwart them in the name of democracy, are separated by deep differences in values, worldview, and definitions of progress. At times it seems that they must be living in wholly different worlds—which, in fact, in many respects they are. Understanding their differences is key to understanding the nature and implications of the profound choices humanity currently faces. . . .

"Citizen movements see a very different reality. Focused on people and the environment, they see the world in a crisis of such magnitude that it threatens the fabric of civilization and the survival of the species—a world of rapidly growing inequality, erosion of relationships of trust and caring, and failing planetary life support systems. Where corporate globalists see the spread of democracy and vibrant market economies, citizen movements see the power to govern shifting away from people and communities to financial speculators and global corporations replacing democracies of people with democracies of money, replacing self-organizing markets with centrally planned corporate economies, and replacing diverse cultures with cultures of greed and materialism."[17]

Alternatives to Economic Globalization and similar critiques offer a daunting array of far-reaching policy and institutional changes: "At the dawn of the twenty-first century, the global corporation stands as the dominant institutional force at the center of human activity and the planet itself. . . . We must dramatically change the publicly traded, limited liability global corporation, just as previous generations set out to eliminate or control the monarchy. Any citizens' agenda for transforming the global economy must be rooted in plans to solve this problem."[18]

They offer a variety of proposals to reform corporate law and governance, assert stronger local control of multinational corporations, and end "corporate–state collusion." They see the need for legislation aimed at three broad goals:

- *Where globalization has encouraged globe-spanning corporate concentration, the course must be reversed.* This can be done by giving priority to smaller businesses capable of functioning as human-scale communities of interest in which people know each other, are dedicated to a common purpose, and that rewards more equitably.

- *Where global corporations now enjoy complete mobility, businesses must be required to be rooted in a place.* They must be owned by people who have direct involvement in the operation—workers, community representatives, suppliers—rather than by distant investors who buy and sell without personal engagement other than profit, growth, and balance sheet figures.

- *All businesses must be transparent and accountable to all stakeholders in the community.* These people bear the ultimate impact of decisions taken. They may include workers, environmentalists, public health officials, human rights activists, and the like. All have suffered from local activities controlled by distant owners.[19]

As one can see, those focused on curbing corporate power view the path ahead not so much one of creating countervailing power at the international level as one of assertive local control. In seeking to shift the bias away from the global to the local, they share the perspective of those advocates for change discussed next.

Bottom-up Change: Beyond Global Governance

Taking the slogan "Think Globally, Act Locally" to heart, a surprisingly diverse array of local organizations and communities are impatient with international processes and are of the view that the way forward is to "just do it" by working toward sustainability in everyday life and in local communities. The Center for a New American Dream, for example, envisions lifestyle changes attractive to some: "[T]he emergence of an alternative in farmers' markets, worker cooperatives, healthy communities, land-use planning, socially responsible businesses, organic cotton, hybrid electric vehicles, barter networks, micro-enterprise, flexible work arrangements, simple living, reduced television watching, environmentally certified wood and fish, and a cultural renaissance of poetry, storytelling, dance, and reconnection to wild places. The new system is being built from the local level up."[20]

In *The Land That Could Be*, William Shutkin discusses what he calls "civic environmentalism" where members of particular geographic or political communities work together to build a future that is environmentally healthy and economically vibrant at the local and regional levels: "Civic environmentalism is the emerging model of social and environmental activism. It is a dynamic and transformative enterprise that moves beyond top-down, centralized law and regulation to planning and implementation at the community and regional levels. It embraces an ecosystem approach to social problem solving, with the environment as both a prime subject and a principal metaphor of civic action. Civic environmentalism does not just focus on specific media or pollutants, as traditional environmental regulation does. Rather, it focuses on the overall health and quality of life of communities— social, economic, and environmental—and the sustainability of that health and quality of life over time. Civic environmentalism links urban, suburban, and rural constituencies in the pursuit of shared goals and visions, and enforces the notion that our fates are bound together by place and time."[21]

In *Global Environmental Politics,* Ronnie Lipschutz searches the landscape for approaches to global environmental protection that might succeed. In most areas he sees severe limitations. "The practice of global environmental politics," he writes, "must be centered elsewhere than the state system, international conferences, agencies, bureaucracies, and centers of corporate capital," all of which he sees as part of the problem. And neither is he happy with mainstream environmental organizations: "But most historians of environmentalism agree that the 1960s marked some kind of watershed in the perception and treatment of the environment, one growing as much out of that decade's tumultuous politics as from the evident damage to nature. Of the many social movements that emerged at that time, environmentalism has become most institutionalized and bureaucratized, the most normalized and mainstreamed, the most connected with 'business as usual.' Indeed, this absorption into the body politic has become something of an obstacle to the practice of environmental politics."[22]

Lipschutz suggests that "those activities that use mainstream methods to accomplish their goals have done little to change the institutions and practices that are the cause of environmental problems in the first place."

In the end Lipschutz finds the wellspring of the new global environmental politics he seeks in action at the local level: "[E]nvironmental problems are, first and foremost, political and, therefore, about power. They have been caused through the exercise of various forms of power and, if they are to be dealt with, it will have to be through the exercise of other forms of power. To exercise such power, we must act collectively, in concert with others. Our actions must be political and have political purpose. We need to understand what politics is missing from our governing systems and restore those missing elements through a new environmental ethics and praxis. . . .

"[A]ctivists must still affect the beliefs and behaviors of real human beings, whose social relations are, for the most part, highly localized. Ideas do not fall from heaven or appear as light bulbs; they must resonate with conditions as experienced and understood by those real human beings, in the places that they live, work, and play. Moreover, it is in those local places that politics, activism, and social power are most intense and engages people most strongly."[23]

There are many ways individuals and communities can exert influence: as citizens and voters, as investors, as consumers, as association members, as workers, as activists, and as educators. In *Red Sky at Morning,* Gus Speth uses these roles to describe how local actions on these fronts can make a global difference. "The biggest threat to our environment is global climate disruption, and the greatest problem in that context is America's energy use and the policies that undergird it. . . . There is no riper target than the U.S. energy scene. And, indeed, the energy–climate problem provides the best example available of how citizen initiative and local action are beginning to address a global-scale problem. . . . We can imagine goals being set for renewable energy use and for reductions in greenhouse gas emissions by businesses and universities, by communities and states, then by groups of states and national associations and organizations of many types, all supported by worried insurers and institutional investors, to the point that local actions are indeed going to scale and changing the world. This is not a distant vision: it is a process that has already begun in the United States. We are not powerless to affect even the most remote and global challenges."[24]

★ ★ ★

This volume began with a thought experiment about planetary stewardship. Over the last 30 years, the international community's actual quest for planetary stewardship has encompassed a variety of intergovernmental, governmental, and civil society initiatives. The results are mixed and generally conceded to be inadequate. The disturbing trends in deterioration continue. A much stronger system of environmental regimes is essential; that is also widely conceded. Those most deeply concerned have looked beyond regimes and asked what else must be done, as we saw in the proceeding section.

Several themes run through these efforts to look beyond regimes for answers:

- The intergovernmental processes that constitute regimes are too closely allied with the forces that gave rise to the problems in the first place to produce real change.

- Real change is only possible if we address the deeper issue of the forces underlying deterioration.

- The search for these underlying drivers leads quickly to institutions and ideas of extraordinary power—the large multinational corporations and their influence on major governments, an unflagging commitment to high rates of economic growth, a consumerist and anthropocentric culture.

- Efforts to change this operating system in fundamental ways are essential, whether through wooing and conversion, creating of powerful new incentives and disincentives, cutting its power centers down to size, or eroding its monopoly through community-based and other bottom-up initiatives.

- None of this is likely unless civil society ascends to new prominence and new roles and engages in a new politics of the global environment. Indeed, explicitly or implicitly, almost all authors reviewed in the section on alternative visions call for a popular movement to drive the changes they see as necessary.

Integral to the transformations that are needed is a change in values—a transition to new habits of thought and a new consciousness captured well in the *Earth Charter:*

We stand at a critical moment in Earth's history, a time when humanity must choose its future. As the world becomes increasingly interdependent and fragile, the future at once holds great peril and great promise. To move forward we must recognize that in the midst of a magnificent diversity of cultures and life forms, we are one human family and one Earth community with a common destiny. We must join together to bring forth a sustainable global society founded on respect for nature, universal human rights, economic justice, and a culture of peace. Towards this end, it is imperative that we, the peoples of Earth, declare our responsibility to one another, to the greater community of life, and to future generations. . . . The spirit of human solidarity and kinship with all life is strengthened when we live with reverence for the mystery of being, gratitude for the gift of life, and humility regarding the human place in nature.[25]

Questions for Discussion

Chapter 1

1. In the thought experiment in the Stewardship Assignments section, what goals, principles, and rules should govern the settlement of pristine Earth? Are the New Delhi Declaration and the Moon Treaty helpful? What more is needed?

2. The authors describe three levels of environmental politics; what are they? Can you think of environmental issues that span two or more of these levels?

3. What is the *tragedy* in Garrett Hardin's "Tragedy of the Commons"? How does it work? Can you think of ways to solve the dilemma?

Chapter 2

1. Can you identify 10 environmental issues that led to the first Earth Day in 1970? In what ways do the 10 threats described in this chapter differ from the Earth Day list? What are the political and policy implications of these differences?

2. Among the 10 challenges discussed in this chapter, how would you compare them in terms of the seriousness and severity of the threat presented? What criteria would you use in ranking them?

3. Can you identify ways in which your own actions and choices contribute to the 10 environmental challenges discussed in this chapter?

4. Which underlying drivers are most important for each of the 10 global threats discussed in this chapter?

5. Having considered the 10 challenges and the underlying drivers, how would you assess prospects for addressing these issues successfully? Our stewardship assignment involves making a transition from a world where these 10 challenges are both real and serious to a world of environmental sustainability and sustainable development. What factors will loom large in determining whether this transition is made successfully?

Chapter 3

1. What do you see as the fault lines or political divides that have recurred throughout the conferences and negotiations reviewed in this chapter? How would you characterize each, and which do you think have been the most important as barriers to concerted international actions?

2. Do you see a pattern in the official titles and subjects of the three main conferences—Stockholm, Rio, and Johannesburg? What is happening to the focus on the environment? What do you think of the concept of sustainable development? Has the concept been good for the environment?

3. Do you agree with the authors' assessment in the final section of this chapter on the question of the letdown after the Rio Earth Summit? Was the Rio process flawed or did external events intervene to change prospects? What lessons might one learn from this experience? Were they applied at Johannesburg?

4. According to the authors, the global challenges tend to have weak domestic constituencies. Why is this so? What are the implications for policy? How can stronger domestic constituencies be built?

Chapter 4

1. What factors and circumstances account for the success of the Montreal Protocol? Compare and contrast these considerations with those associated with the climate treaty.

2. What do you make of the apparent disagreement between your two coauthors in the passages quoted in this chapter? Who is right? What criteria should be used to determine whether a treaty or policy has been successful? What needs to happen for a regime to count as a success?

3. As noted, despite more than a decade of discussion of the issue, there is still no treaty on world forests or deforestation. Why do you think this is the case? Are there features that make it particularly problematic? What would such a treaty look like were it negotiated today? Do you think the relevant international NGO community is still advocating commencement of negotiations toward such a treaty?

4. Both the climate treaty and the POPs treaty explicitly incorporate the Precautionary Principle. What is the significance of its inclusion? The principle is highly controversial. Can you sketch the arguments on both sides?

Chapter 5

1. It has been noted that no one can understand the United Nations' organizational structure because it does not make sense. In our concentric circles, the principal environmental focus is where? Where is health? Education? Trade? Does it matter? Is

environment marginalized within the UN? Is the public invisibility of the UN's role in global environmental governance a liability or an asset?

2. The development assistance agencies in general and the World Bank in particular have been the subject of recurring criticism for their environmental performance. In 2004 a panel headed by Emil Salim, former environment minister in Indonesia, recommended to the World Bank that, in light of the global warming threat, it should steer away from funding fossil fuel–based development. The proposal was rejected by the Bank. Should it have been? The World Bank has never made loans for nuclear power development. Should it?

3. What considerations are motivating many private business corporations in the United States to reduce their greenhouse gas emissions even though they are not legally required to do so? How much change can be driven by these factors?

Chapter 6

1. Are you a market liberal cornucopian, an institutional reformist, a neo-Malthusian bioenvironmentalist, or a social green? Why? What are the strong and weak points in each of these perspectives or worldviews?

2. Of the various ways of reforming and strengthening the current system of international environmental regimes, which do you think would make the biggest difference? Why?

3. Of the five "alternative visions" presented in the chapter, which would have the biggest impacts on reversing current trends in global environmental deterioration? Which have realistic prospects of actual adoption today? In the future?

4. If you had been in charge of planetary stewardship over the past three decades, what would you have done differently?

References

Chapter I

1. International Law Association. April 2002. New Delhi Declaration of Principles of International Law Relating to Sustainable Development. Resolution 3/2002.
2. See http://untreaty.un.org.
3. Osborn, F. 1948. *Our Plundered Planet*. Boston: Little, Brown, 108–111, 188.
4. McNeill, J. R. 2000. *Something New Under the Sun*. New York: W. W. Norton, 4, 16.

Chapter 2

1. Rowland, S. and M. Molina. 1974. Stratospheric sink for chlorofluoromethanes: Chlorine catalysed destruction of ozone. *Nature* 249:810.
2. McKibben, W. 1999. *The End of Nature*. New York: Doubleday.
3. Lubchenco, J. 1998. Entering the century of the environment. *Science* 279:492.
4. The statement is reprinted in *Renewable Resources Journal*, Summer 2001:16.
5. Vitousek, P. M., et al. 1997. Human domination of Earth's ecosystems. *Science* 277:494.
6. National Research Council. 2001. *Climate Change Science: An Analysis of Some Key Questions*. Washington, D.C.: National Academies Press, 3, 18.
7. National Research Council. 2002. *Abrupt Climate Change: Inevitable Surprises*. Washington, D.C.: National Academies Press, 1.
8. Gagosian, R. B. 27 January 2003. Abrupt climate change: Should we be worried? Woods Hole Oceanographic Institution, 8.
9. Arctic Climate Impact Assessment. 2004. *Impacts of a Warming Arctic*. Cambridge: Cambridge University Press, 10.
10. UNESCO et al. *Water for People: Water for Life*. Executive Summary, 33.
11. Carson, R. 1962. *Silent Spring*. Boston: Houghton Mifflin, 15.
12. See the reports collected by the Center for Children's Health and the Environment, Mount Sinai School of Medicine, at www.childenvironment.org.
13. Wilson, E. O. 1992. *The Diversity of Life*. Cambridge, Mass.: Harvard University Press, 12.
14. United Nations. 1982. *World Charter for Nature*. www.un.org/documents/ga/res/37/a37r007.htm.

15. Cowling, E., et al. Optimizing nitrogen management in food and energy production and environmental protection. Summary statement from the Second International Nitrogen Conference, December 2001; See also Driscoll, C. et al. 2003. Nitrogen pollution, *Environment*. September, 8.
16. Smil, V. 1993. *Global Ecology*. London: Routledge, 35.
17. Hunter, D., et al. 2002. *International Environmental Law and Policy*. New York: Foundation Press, 54–55.

Chapter 3

1. Gandhi, I. 1982. *Peoples and Problems*. London: Hodder and Stoughton; see also Gandhi, I. 1984. *Indira Gandhi on Environment*. Department of Environment, Government of India.
2. The texts of most declarations and treaties discussed in this book can be found in Hunter, D., et al. 2002. *International Environmental Law and Policy: Treaty Supplement*. New York: Foundation Press.
3. National Research Council. 1979. *Carbon Dioxide and Climate*. Washington, D.C.: National Academy of Sciences.
4. Khor, M. 2001. Globalization and sustainable development. *International Review for Environmental Strategies* 2(2):210.
5. Cassidy, J. 2005. The ringleader. *New Yorker*, August 1, 42.

Chapter 4

1. Hunter, D., et al. 2002. *International Environmental Law and Policy*. New York: Foundation Press, 272–73.
2. Levy, D. and P. Newell. 2000. Oceans apart: Business responses to global environmental issues in Europe and the United States. *Environment* 42(9):9.
3. Porter, G., et al. 2000. *Global Environmental Politics*. Boulder, Colo.: Westview Press, 71.
4. This discussion is based on Hovi, J., et al. 2003. The Oslo–Potsdam solution to measuring regime effectiveness. *Global Environmental Politics* 3(3):74.
5. Haas, P. M. 2001. Environment: Pollution. In *Managing Global Issues: Lessons Learned*, ed. P. J. Simmons and C. deJonge Oudraat. Washington, D.C.: Carnegie Endowment for International Peace, 310.
6. Birnie, P. and A. Boyle. 2002. *International Law and the Environment*. Oxford: Oxford University Press, 752.
7. Speth, J. G. 2004. International environmental law: Can it deal with the big issues? *Vermont Law Review* 28(3):780; See also Speth, J. G. 2005. *Red Sky at Morning: America and the Crisis of the Global Environment*. New Haven: Yale University Press.
8. Downie, D. L. 2005. Global environmental policy: Governance through regimes. In *The Global Environment: Institutions, Law and Policy*, ed. R. S. Axelrod et al. Washington, D.C.: CQ Press, 64.
9. Paehlke, R. C. 2003. *Democracy's Dilemma: Environment, Social Equity and the Global Economy*. Cambridge, Mass.: MIT Press, 208.
10. Clapp, J. 2001. *Toxic Exports*. Ithaca: Cornell University Press, 3.
11. Speth, J. G. 2005. Afterword. In *Red Sky at Morning: America and the Crisis of the Global Environment*. New Haven: Yale University Press, 203.

Chapter 5

1. Esty, D. 2002. The World Trade Organization's legitimacy crisis. *World Trade Review* 1(1):7–22; 2001. Bridging the trade–environment divide. *Journal of Economic Perspectives* 15(3):113–130; and 1994. *Greening the GATT: Trade, Environment and the Future.* Washington, D.C.: Institute for International Economics.

2. Cashore, B. 2002. Legitimacy and the privatization of environmental governance: How non-state market-driven (NSMD) governance systems gain rule-making authority. *Governance* 15:504.

3. Cashore, B., et al., 2004. *Governing through Markets: Forest Certification and the Emergence of Nonstate Authority.* New Haven: Yale University Press; Cashore, B., et al., eds. 2003. *Confronting Sustainability: Forest Certification in Developing and Transitioning Societies.* New Haven: Yale School of Forestry and Environmental Studies.

Chapter 6

1. The four worldviews described here are those developed by Clapp, J. and P. Dauvergne. 2005. *Paths to a Green World: The Political Economy of the Global Environment.* Cambridge, Mass.: MIT Press, 3; see also Haas, Peter M. 2002. Constructing environmental security from resource scarcity. *Global Environmental Politics* 2(1):1–19.

2. The discussion here draws on Haas, P. M. et al., eds. 1995. *Institutions for the Earth: Sources of Effective International Environmental Protection.* Cambridge, Mass.: MIT Press, 3–24. See also Weiss, E. B. and Jacobson, H., eds. 1998. *Engaging Countries: Strengthening Compliance with International Environmental Accords.* Cambridge, Mass.: MIT Press, 4–12; Victor, D. G., et al., eds. 1998. *The Implementation and Effectiveness of International Environmental Commitment.* Cambridge, Mass.: MIT Press, 6–8; Young, O. R., ed. 1999. *The Effectiveness of International Environmental Regimes.* Cambridge, Mass.: MIT Press, 19–28; and Speth, J. G. 2005. *Red Sky at Morning: America and the Crisis of the Global Environment.* New Haven: Yale University Press.

3. Florini, A. 2003. *The Coming Democracy: New Rules for Running a New World.* Washington, D.C.: Island Press, 14–15.

4. Rischard, J. F. 2002. *High Noon: 20 Global Problems, 20 Years to Solve Them.* New York: Basic Books, 177–178.

5. Wapner, P. 1996. *Environmental Activism and World Civic Politics.* Albany: State University of New York Press, 2–3.

6. Slaughter, A.-M. 2004. *A New World Order.* Princeton: Princeton University Press, 4.

7. Brown, L. R. 2003. *Plan B: Rescuing a Planet under Stress and a Civilization in Trouble.* New York: W. W. Norton, 176.

8. Speth, J. G. 2005. *Red Sky at Morning: America and the Crisis of the Global Environment.* New Haven: Yale University Press, 157.

9. Ehrlich, P. and A. Ehrlich. 2004. *One with Nineveh: Politics, Consumption and the Human Future.* Washington, D.C.: Island Press, 2004, 215.

10. *Red Sky at Morning,* 162.

11. Hawken, P., et al. 1999. *Natural Capitalism.* Boston: Little, Brown, 260–61.

12. *Natural Capitalism,* 320–21.

13. Daly, H. and J. Farley. 2004. *Ecological Economics.* Washington, D.C.: Island Press, 6, 23.

14. The International Forum on Globalization. 2002. *Alternatives to Economic Globalization: A Better World Is Possible.* San Francisco: Berrett-Koehler, 17–20.

15. *Alternatives to Economic Globalization*, 61–62.
16. *Alternatives to Economic Globalization*, 8.
17. *Alternatives to Economic Globalization*, 4–5.
18. *Alternatives to Economic Globalization*, 122.
19. *Alternatives to Economic Globalization*, 145–46.
20. Schor, J. B. and B. Taylor. 2002. *Sustainable Planet: Solutions for the Twenty-first Century.* Boston: Beacon Press, xi.
21. Shutkin, W. A. 2000. *The Land That Could Be.* Cambridge, Mass.: MIT Press, 238.
22. Lipschutz, R. D. 2004. *Global Environmental Politics.* Washington, D.C.: CQ Press, 133.
23. *Global Environmental Politics,* 226, 175.
24. *Red Sky at Morning,* 204.
25. Earth Charter Initiative, www.earthcharter.org.

Further Reading

Chapter 1

Barkin, S. J. and G. Shambaugh. 1999. *Anarchy and the Environment*. Albany: State University of New York Press.

Diamond, J. 2005. *Collapse: How Societies Choose to Fail or Succeed*. New York: Viking.

Gardner, G.T. and Paul C. Stern. 2002. *Environmental Problems and Human Behavior*. Boston: Pearson.

Gore, A. 1993. *Earth in the Balance*. New York: Penguin.

Hay, P. 2002. *Main Currents of Western Environmental Thought*. Bloomington: Indiana University Press.

Kellert, S. K. and T. J. Farnham, eds. 2002. *The Good in Nature and Humanity*. Washington, D.C.: Island Press.

Lee, K. N. 1993. *Compass and Gyroscope*. Washington, D.C.: Island Press.

Marten, G. G. 2001. *Human Ecology*. London: Earthscan.

McNeill, J. R. 2000. *Something New Under the Sun*. New York: W.W. Norton.

Milbrath, L. W. 1996. *Learning to Think Environmentally While There Is Still Time*. Albany: State University of New York Press.

Osborn, F. 1948. *Our Plundered Planet*. Boston: Little, Brown.

Ostrom, E. 1990. *Governing the Commons*. Cambridge: Cambridge University Press.

Saunier R. and R. Meganck. 2004. *C. H. A. O. S. S.: An Essay and Glossary for Students and Practitioners of Global Environmental Governance*. London: A. A. Balkema Publishers.

Shabecoff, P. 2000. *Earth Rising: American Environmentalism in the Twenty-First Century*. Washington, D.C.: Island Press.

Shabecoff, P. 2003. *A Fierce Green Fire: The American Environmental Movement*. Washington, D.C.: Island Press.

Singer, P. 2003. *One World*. New Haven: Yale University Press.

Speth, J. G., ed. 2003. *Worlds Apart: Globalization and the Environment*. Washington, D.C.: Island Press.

Chapter 2

Arctic Climate Impact Assessment. 2004. *Impacts of a Warming Arctic.* Cambridge: Cambridge University Press.

Benedick, R. E. 1998. *Ozone Diplomacy: New Directions in Safeguarding the Planet.* Cambridge, Mass.: Harvard University Press.

Carson, R. 1962. *Silent Spring.* Boston: Houghton Mifflin.

Claussen, E., ed. 2001. *Climate Change: Science, Strategies and Solutions.* Boston: E.J. Brill.

Colborn, T., et al. 1996. *Our Stolen Future.* New York: Dutton.

Davis, D. 2002. *When Smoke Ran Like Water.* New York: Basic Books.

Gleick, P. 2004. *The World's Water.* Washington, D.C.: Island Press.

Harrison, P. and F. Pearce. 2000. *AAAS Atlas of Population and Environment.* Berkeley: University of California Press.

Hollander, J. M. 2003. *The Real Environmental Crisis.* Berkeley: University of California Press.

Hunter, D., et al. 2002. *International Environmental Law and Policy.* New York: Foundation Press, 54–55.

Kellert, S. R. 1996. *The Value of Life: Biological Diversity and Human Society.* Washington, D.C.: Island Press.

Levin, S. 1999. *Fragile Dominion: Complexity and the Commons.* Reading, Mass.: Perseus Books.

Linden E. 1998. *The Future in Plain Sight: Nine Clues to the Coming Instability.* New York: Simon and Schuster.

Lomborg, B. 2001. *The Skeptical Environmentalist.* Cambridge: Cambridge University Press.

McKibben, W. 1999. *The End of Nature.* New York: Doubleday.

Meadows, D., J. Ronders, and Dennis Meadows. 2004. *Limits to Growth Re: 30 Year Update.* White River Junction, UT: Chelsea Green.

Millennium Ecoystem Assessment. 2005. *Ecosystems and Human Well-Being.* Vols. 1–4. Washington, D.C.: Island Press.

Millennium Ecosystem Assessment. 2005. *Ecosystems and Human Well-Being: Synthesis.* Washington, D.C.: Island Press.

Myers, N. and J. Kent. 2005. *The New Gaia Atlas of Planetary Management.* London: Gaia Books.

National Assessment Synthesis Team. 2000. *Climate Change Impacts on the Untied States.* New York: Cambridge University Press.

National Research Council. 1999. *Our Common Journey: A Transition Toward Sustainability.* Washington, D.C.: National Academies Press.

National Research Council. 2001. *Climate Change Science: An Analysis of Some Key Questions.* Washington, D.C.: National Academies Press.

National Research Council. 2002. *Abrupt Climate Change: Inevitable Surprises.* Washington, D.C.: National Academies Press, 1.

Organization for Economic Co-operation and Development. 2001. *OECD Environmental Outlook.* Paris: OECD.

Pauly, D. and J. Maclean. 2003. *In a Perfect Ocean: The State of Fisheries in the North Atlantic Ocean.* Washington, D.C.: Island Press.

Pew Oceans Commission. 2003. *America's Living Oceans: Charting a Course for a Sea Change.* Arlington, Va.: Pew Oceans Commission.

Pirages, D. and K. Cousins. 2005. *From Resource Scarcity to Ecological Security.* Cambridge, Mass.: MIT Press.

Raven, P. H. and L. R. Berg. 2004. *Environment.* Fort Worth, Texas: Harcourt College.

Repetto, R. and M. Gillis. 1988. *Public Policies and the Misuse of Forest Resources.* Cambridge: Cambridge University Press.

Safina, C. 1997. *Song for the Blue Ocean.* New York: Henry Holt & Co.

Smil, V. 1993. *Global Ecology.* London: Routledge.

Speth, J. G. 2005. *Red Sky at Morning: America and the Crisis of the Global Environment.* New Haven: Yale University Press.

United Nations Development Programme. Annual series. *Human Development Report.* New York: Oxford University Press.

United Nations Environment Programme et al. 1998. *Protecting Our Planet, Securing Our Future.* Nairobi, Kenya, and Washington, D.C.: The World Bank.

United Nations Environment Programme. 2002. *Global Environmental Outlook 3.* London: Earthscan.

United Nations Environment Programme et al. 2005. *One Planet, Many People: Atlas of Our Changing Environment.* Nairobi, Kenya: UNEP.

Wargo, J. 1998. *Our Children's Toxic Legacy: How Science and Law Fail to Protect Us from Pesticides.* New Haven: Yale University Press.

Weiss, E.B. 1989. *In Fairness to Future Generations.* Tokyo: United Nations University Press.

Wilson, E. O. 1992. *The Diversity of Life.* Cambridge, Mass.: Harvard University Press.

Wilson, E. O. 2002. *The Future of Life.* New York: Alfred A. Knopf.

Woodwell, G. 2001. *Forests in a Full World.* New Haven: Yale University Press.

World Bank. 2003. *Sustainable Development in a Dynamic World: World Development Report 2003.* New York: Oxford University Press.

World Resources Institute et al. *World Resources.* Washington, D.C.: World Resources Institute. Biennial series.

World Wildlife Fund International, et al. 2004. *Living Planet Report 2004.* Gland, Switzerland: WWF International.

Worldwatch Institute. Annual series. *Vital Signs: The Trends That Are Shaping Our Future.* New York: W. W. Norton.

Chapter 3

Agarwal, A., et al., eds. 2001. *Poles Apart.* New Delhi: Center for Science and the Environment.

Agyeman, J., et al., eds. 2003. *Just Sustainabilities: Development in an Unequal World.* Cambridge, Mass.: MIT Press.

Anand, R. 2004. *International Environmental Justice: A North–South Dimension.* Hampshire, England: Ashgate Publishing.

Caldwell, L. 1996. *International Environmental Policy.* Durham, N.C.: Duke University Press.

Choucri, N., ed. 1993. *Global Accord.* Cambridge, Mass.: MIT Press.

Gandhi, I. 1982. *Peoples and Problems.* London: Hodder and Stoughton.

Harris, P. G. 2001. *International Equity and Global Environmental Politics.* Hampshire, England: Ashgate Publishing.

Hunter, D., et al. 2002. *International Environmental Law and Policy.* New York: Foundation Press.

162 GLOBAL ENVIRONMENTAL GOVERNANCE

Miller, M. A. 1995. *The Third World in Global Environmental Politics*. Boulder, Col.: Lynne Rienner.

Mirovitskaya, N. and W. Ascher. 2001. *Guide to Sustainable Development and Environmental Policy*. Durham, N.C.: Duke University Press.

National Research Council. 1979. *Carbon Dioxide and Climate*. Washington, D.C.: National Academy of Sciences.

Shabecoff, P. 1996. *A New Name for Peace: International Environmentalism, Sustainable Development, and Democracy*. Hanover, N.H.: University Press of New England.

Strong, M. 2001. *Where on Earth Are We Going?* New York: Texere.

Tolba, M. 1998. *Global Environmental Diplomacy*. Cambridge, Mass.: MIT Press.

Train, R. E. 2003. *Politics, Pollution and Pandas: An Environmental Memoir*. Washington, D.C.: Island Press.

Chapter 4

Anderson, S. O. and K. M. Sarma. 2002. *Protecting the Ozone Layer*. London: Earthscan.

Axelrod, R. S., et al., eds. 2005. *The Global Environment Institutions, Law and Policy*. Washington, D.C.: CQ Press.

Benedick, R. E. 1998. *Ozone Diplomacy: New Directions in Safeguarding the Planet*. Cambridge, Mass.: Harvard University Press.

Birnie, P. and A. Boyle. 2002. *International Law and the Environment*. Oxford: Oxford University Press.

Bocking, S. 2004. *Nature's Experts: Science, Politics and the Environment*. New Brunswick, N.J.: Rutgers University Press.

Clapp, J. 2001. *Toxic Exports*. Ithaca: Cornell University Press.

DeSombre, E. R. 2000. *Domestic Sources of International Environmental Policy*. Cambridge, Mass.: MIT Press.

DiMento, J. F. C. 2003. *The Global Environment and International Law*. Austin: University of Texas Press.

Gelbspan, R. 2004. *Boiling Point*. New York: Basic Books.

Geller, H. 2003. *Energy Revolution: Policies for a Sustainable Future*. Washington, D.C.: Island Press.

Glantz, M. H. 2003. *Climate Affairs*. Washington, D.C.: Island Press.

Haas, Peter M. 1990. *Saving the Mediterranean*. New York: Columbia University Press.

Hampson, F. and J. Reppy, eds. 1996. *Earthly Goods*. Ithaca: Cornell University Press.

Hempel, L. C. 1996. *Environmental Governance: The Global Challenge*. Washington, D.C.: Island Press.

Hunter, D., et al. 2002. *International Environmental Law and Policy*. New York: Foundation Press, 272–73.

Kennedy, D. and J. A. Riggs. 2000. *U.S. Policy and the Global Environment*. Washington, D.C.: The Aspen Institute.

Litfin, K. 1994. *Ozone Discourses*. New York: Columbia University Press.

Paehlke, R. C. 2003. *Democracy's Dilemma: Environment, Social Equity and the Global Economy*. Cambridge, Mass.: MIT Press, 208.

Parson, E. A. 2003. *Protecting the Ozone Layer*. Oxford: Oxford University Press.

Porter, G., et al. 2000. *Global Environmental Politics*. Boulder, Colo.: Westview Press.

Schneider, S. H., et al., eds. 2002. *Climate Change Policy*. Washington, D.C.: Island Press.

Schreurs, M. and E. Economy. 1997. *The Internationalization of Environmental Protection*. Cambridge: Cambridge University Press.

Simmons, P. J. and C. dej. Oudraat, eds. 2001. *Managing Global Issues: Lessons Learned*. Washington, D.C.: Carnegie Endowment for International Peace.

Speth, J. G. 2005. *Red Sky at Morning: America and the Crisis of the Global Environment*. New Haven: Yale University Press.

Stewart, R. B. and J. B. Wiener. 2003. *Reconstructing Climate Policy*. Washington, D.C.: The AEI Press.

Victor, D. 2004. *Climate Change: Debating America's Policy Options*. New York: Council on Foreign Relations.

Chapter 5

Bojö, J. and K.-G. Mäler. 1990. *Environment and Development: An Economic Approach*. Boston: Kluwer Academic Publishers.

Cashore, B., et al., 2004. *Governing through Markets: Forest Certification and the Emergence of Nonstate Authority*. New Haven: Yale University Press.

Dasgupta, P. 2001. *Human Well-Being and the Natural Environment*. Oxford: Oxford University Press.

Dodds, F. 2004. *How to Lobby at Intergovernmental Meetings*. London: Earthscan.

Esty, D. 1994. *Greening the GATT: Trade, Environment, and the Future*. Washington, D.C.: Institute for International Economics.

Holliday, C. O., et al. 2002. *Walking the Talk: The Business Case for Sustainable Development*. San Francisco: Berrett-Koehler Publishers.

Interaction. Annual. *The Reality of Aid: An Independent Review of International Aid*. London: Earthscan.

Johnson, P. M. and A. Beaulieu. 1996. *The Environment and NAFTA*. Washington, D.C.: Island Press.

Kanie, N. and P. M. Haas, eds. 2004. *Emerging Forces in Environmental Governance*. Tokyo: United Nations University Press.

Keohane, R. O. and M. A. Levy. 1996. *Institutions for Environmental Aid*. Cambridge, Mass: MIT Press.

Lipschutz, R. 1996. *Global Civil Society and Global Environmental Governance*. Albany: State University of New York Press.

National Research Council. 2002. *New Tools for Environmental Protection*. Washington, D.C.: National Academies Press.

New Zealand Ministry of Foreign Affairs and Trade. Annual. *United Nations Handbook*. Wellington, New Zealand.

Singh, N. and V. Titi. 1995. *Empowerment: towards Sustainable Development*. London: Zed Books.

Speth, J. G. 2003. *Worlds Apart: Globalization and the Environment*. Washington, D.C.: Island Press.

Thomas, V., et al. 2000. *The Quality of Growth*. New York: Oxford University Press.

United Nations Development Programme. 2002. *Capacity for Development: New Solutions to Old Problems*. London: Earthscan.

Wapner, P. 1996. *Environmental Activism and World Civic Politics*. Albany: State University of New York Press.

World Resource Institute. 2005. *The Wealthy of the Poor: Managing Ecosystems to Fight Poverty.* Washington, D.C.: World Resources Institute.

Young, O. R., ed. 1997. *Global Governance: Drawing Insights from the Environmental Experience.* Cambridge, Mass.: MIT Press.

Zaelke, D., et al., eds. 1993. *Trade and the Environment.* Washington, D.C.: Island Press.

Chapter 6

Biermann, F. and S. Bauer. 2005. *A World Environment Organization.* Burlington, Vt.: Ashgate Publishing.

Brown, L. R. 2003. *Plan B: Rescuing a Planet under Stress and a Civilization in Trouble.* New York: W.W. Norton.

Chambers, W. B. and J. F. Green. 2005. *Reforming International Environmental Governance.* Tokyo: United Nations University Press.

Clapp, J. and P. Dauvergne. 2005. *Paths to a Green World: The Political Economy of the Global Environment.* Cambridge, Mass.: MIT Press.

Daly, H. and J. Farley. 2004. *Ecological Economics.* Washington, D.C.: Island Press, 6, 23.

DeGraaf, J., et al. 2002. *Affluenza.* San Francisco: Berrett-Koehler Publishers.

Dryzek, J. S. 1997. *The Politics of the Earth.* Oxford: Oxford University Press.

Edwards, A. R. 2005. *The Sustainability Revolution.* British Columbia: New Society Publishers.

Ehrlich, P. and A. Ehrlich. 2004. *One with Nineveh: Politics, Consumption and the Human Future.* Washington, D.C.: Island Press.

Esty, D. and M. Ivanova. 2002. *Global Environmental Governance: Options and Opportunities.* New Haven: Yale School of Forestry & Environmental Studies.

Florini, A. 2003. *The Coming Democracy: New Rules for Running a New World.* Washington, D.C.: Island Press.

Haas, P. M., et al., eds. 1995. *Institutions for the Earth: Sources of Effective International Environmental Protection.* Cambridge, Mass.: MIT Press.

Hammond, A. 1998. *Which World? Scenarios for the 21st Century.* Washington, D.C.: Island Press.

Hawken, P., et al. 1999. *Natural Capitalism.* Boston: Little, Brown.

International Forum on Globalization. 2002. *Alternatives to Economic Globalization: A Better World Is Possible.* San Francisco: Berrett-Koehler.

Ivanova, M. 2005. *Can the Anchor Hold? Rethinking the United Nations Environment Programme for the 21st Century.* New Haven: Yale School of Forestry & Environmental Studies.

Kanie, N. and P. Haas. 2004. *Emerging Forces in Environmental Governance.* Tokyo: UN University Press.

Kellert, S. K. 2005. *Building for Life: Designing and Understanding the Human-Nature Connection.* Washington, D.C.: Island Press.

Korten, D. C. 1999. *The Post-corporate World.* San Francisco: Berrett-Koehle Publishers.

Lipschutz, R. D. 2004. *Global Environmental Politics.* Washington, D.C.: CQ Press.

Malone, L. and S. Pasternack. 2006. *Defending the Environment: Strategies to Enforce Environmental International Law.* Washington, D.C.: Island Press.

Myers, N. and J. Kent. 2001. *Perverse Subsidies.* Washington, D.C.: Island Press.

Myers, N. and J. Kent. 2004. *The New Consumers: The Influence of Affluence on the Environment.* Washington, D.C.: Island Press.

Olson, R. and D. Rejeski. 2005. *Environmentalism and the Technologies of Tomorrow.* Washington, D.C.: Island Press.

Panayotou, T. 1998. *Instruments of Change: Motivating and Financing Sustainable Development.* London: Earthscan.

Raskin, P., et al. 2002. *Great Transition.* Boston: Tellus Institute and Stockholm Environment Institute.

Rischard, J. F. 2002. *High Noon: 20 Global Problems, 20 Years to Solve Them.* New York: Basic Books.

Schor, J. B. and B. Taylor. 2002. *Sustainable Planet: Solutions for the Twenty-first Century.* Boston: Beacon Press.

Shutkin, W. A. 2000. *The Land That Could Be.* Cambridge, Mass.: MIT Press.

Slaughter, A.-M. 2004. *A New World Order.* Princeton: Princeton University Press, 4.

Speth, J. G. 2004. *Red Sky at Morning: America and the Crisis of the Global Environment.* New Haven: Yale University Press.

Susskind, L. E. 1994. *Environmental Diplomacy: Negotiating More Effective Environmental Agreements.* Oxford: Oxford University Press.

Victor, D. G., et al., eds. 1998. *The Implementation and Effectiveness of International Environmental Commitment.* Cambridge, Mass.: MIT Press.

Vig, N. J. and M. G. Faure. 2004. *Green Giants: Environmental Policies of the United States and the European Union.* Cambridge, Mass.: MIT Press.

Weiss, E. B. and Jacobson, H., eds. 1998. *Engaging Countries: Strengthening Compliance with International Environmental Accords.* Cambridge, Mass.: MIT Press.

Wapner, P. 1996. *Environmental Activism and World Civic Politics.* Albany: State University of New York Press.

Young, O. R., ed. 1999. *The Effectiveness of International Environmental Regimes.* Cambridge, Mass.: MIT Press.

Zaelke, D., et al., eds. 2005. *Making Law Work: Environmental Compliance and Sustainable Development.* London: Cameron May.

Online Resources

Global Response, http://globalresponse.org

Center for International Earth Science Information Network, http://www.ciesin.org

World Resources Institute Earthtrends Environment Information, http://www.earthtrends.wri.org

UNEP Global Environment Outlet data Portal, http://geodata.grid.unep.ch

International Environmental Law, http://www.ecolex.org

International Institute for Sustainable Development reporting on international environmental agreements. http://www.iisd.ca/linkages

International Institute for Sustainable Development library of Sustainable Development materials, http://www.iisd.org/ic

European Acid Rain website, http://www.unece.org/env/lrtap

International Environmental Agreements database, http://iea.uoregon.edu

International Waterlaw for river basins, http://www.internationalwaterlaw.org

World Business Council for Sustainable Development, http://www.wbcsd.org

European Environment Agency, http://www.eea.eu.int/main_html

Index

World Meteorological Organization, 65
World Summit on Sustainable Development
(WSSD) in 2002, 53, 76–78
World Trade Organization (WTO), 31, 75,
120–21, 131, 141
Worldviews and environmental policies,
125–27

Worldwatch Institute, 64
World Water Development Report (2003), 35
World Wildlife Fund, 123
Worm, Boris, 36

Yellow River, 34
Yellowstone National Park, 62